1,000,000 Books

are available to read at

www.ForgottenBooks.com

Read online
Download PDF
Purchase in print

ISBN 978-1-333-51858-5
PIBN 10514534

This book is a reproduction of an important historical work. Forgotten Books uses state-of-the-art technology to digitally reconstruct the work, preserving the original format whilst repairing imperfections present in the aged copy. In rare cases, an imperfection in the original, such as a blemish or missing page, may be replicated in our edition. We do, however, repair the vast majority of imperfections successfully; any imperfections that remain are intentionally left to preserve the state of such historical works.

Forgotten Books is a registered trademark of FB &c Ltd.
Copyright © 2018 FB &c Ltd.
FB &c Ltd, Dalton House, 60 Windsor Avenue, London, SW19 2RR.
Company number 08720141. Registered in England and Wales.

For support please visit www.forgottenbooks.com

1 MONTH OF FREE READING

at

www.ForgottenBooks.com

By purchasing this book you are eligible for one month membership to ForgottenBooks.com, giving you unlimited access to our entire collection of over 1,000,000 titles via our web site and mobile apps.

To claim your free month visit: www.forgottenbooks.com/free514534

* Offer is valid for 45 days from date of purchase. Terms and conditions apply.

English
Français
Deutsche
Italiano
Español
Português

www.forgottenbooks.com

Mythology Photography **Fiction**
Fishing Christianity **Art** Cooking
Essays Buddhism Freemasonry
Medicine **Biology** Music **Ancient Egypt** Evolution Carpentry Physics
Dance Geology **Mathematics** Fitness
Shakespeare **Folklore** Yoga Marketing
Confidence Immortality Biographies
Poetry **Psychology** Witchcraft
Electronics Chemistry History **Law**
Accounting **Philosophy** Anthropology
Alchemy Drama Quantum Mechanics
Atheism Sexual Health **Ancient History**
Entrepreneurship Languages Sport
Paleontology Needlework Islam
Metaphysics Investment Archaeology
Parenting Statistics Criminology
Motivational

PARISH COUNCILS

A Handbook to the
LOCAL GOVERNMENT ACT, 1894

BY

PORTLAND B. AKERMAN

(Solicitor of the Supreme Court)

AND

PERCY H. FORD

LONDON
GEORGE ROUTLEDGE & SONS, Limited
BROADWAY, LUDGATE HILL
MANCHESTER AND NEW YORK

THE LIBRARY
OF
THE UNIVERSITY
OF CALIFORNIA
LOS ANGELES

THE
LOCAL GOVERNMENT ACT
1894

MR. HOLDSWORTH'S LEGAL HANDBOOKS.

In Crown 8vo, 640 pp., 5s.

THE PRACTICAL FAMILY LAWYER.

In Crown 8vo, 2s. 6d. each.

THE HANDY BOOK OF PARISH LAW.
THE NEW COUNTY COURT GUIDE.

In Fcap. 8vo, 1s. each.

LANDLORD AND TENANT.
WILLS AND EXECUTORS.
THE BALLOT ACT.
MASTER AND SERVANT.
WEIGHTS AND MEASURES.
THE MARRIED WOMEN'S PROPERTY ACT.
THE BANKRUPTCY ACT, 1883
THE AGRICULTURAL HOLDINGS ACT, 1883, ETC.
THE CORRUPT AND ILLEGAL PRACTICES PREVENTION ACT, 1883.
THE ALLOTMENTS ACTS, 1887.
THE LOCAL GOVERNMENT ACT, 1888.

PARISH COUNCILS

A HANDBOOK

TO THE

Local Government Act 1894

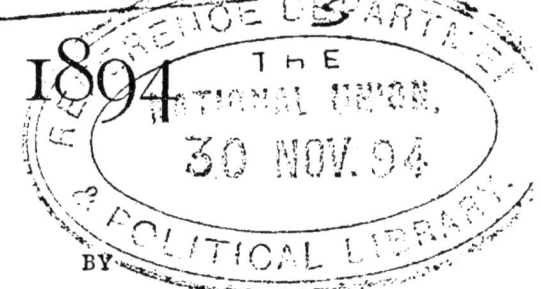

BY

PORTLAND B. AKERMAN
(*Solicitor of the Supreme Court*)

AND

PERCY H. FORD

SECOND EDITION.

LONDON
GEORGE ROUTLEDGE & SONS, Limited
Broadway, Ludgate Hill
MANCHESTER AND NEW YORK
1894

LONDON:
PRINTED BY WOODFALL AND KINDER,
70 TO 76, LONG ACRE, W.C.

PREFACE.

—o—

THE Local Government Act, 1894, commonly called the "Parish Councils Act," introduces changes in the local government of the country so little short of revolutionary, that to attempt anything like an exhaustive treatment of the subject in a work of this character would only result in failure. Our aim has been to place before our readers, in a clear and intelligible form, a general statement of the effect of the Act, and, if possible, to induce that fuller interest in local administration which it is the object of the measure to create.

With this view we have abstained as much as possible from merely technical details, to which full justice could be done only in a work of much greater size. But we trust that our Introduction, coupled with the notes appended to the various clauses of the Act, will be found to elucidate some of its complexities, and to furnish the very numerous class who are desirous of information as to its provisions with a sufficient aid to an intelligent appreciation of their scope and character. A more truly democratic measure, one more national in the belief which underlies it, that Englishmen are endowed with the faculty of self-government, it would be difficult to conceive, and there can be no doubt that it will take rank with what is known as the "County Councils Act of 1888," as one of the most important extensions of local government of modern times.

We desire to take this opportunity of acknowledging that for the concise statement of the qualification of parochial electors, which will be found at page 20, we are indebted to the kindness of Mr. J. Renwick Seager, the author of several well-known works on election law, and that for some valuable suggestions we owe our sincere thanks to Sir Charles W. Dilke, Bart., M.P., who has with great courtesy obliged us by perusing the major portion of our proof sheets and expressed his warm approval of the work.

Portland B. Akerman.
Percy H. Ford.

Temple Chambers,
    Temple Avenue, E.C.
        March, 1894.

CONTENTS.

—o—

THE LOCAL GOVERNMENT ACT, 1894.

(56 & 57 Vict. c. 73.)

	PAGE
INTRODUCTION.	13
Parish Meetings	20
Qualification of Parochial Electors	20
Parish Councils	28
The "Adoptive Acts"	42
Acquisition of land for Allotments, etc.	45
Public property and Charities	48
Special provisions as to small rural Parishes	56
Guardians	62
District Councils	68
Application of Act to Boroughs	84
Application of Act to London	85
Conduct of Elections, etc.	90
Simplification of Areas	94
Powers of County Council	97
Audit of Accounts	99
Existing Officers	100
Commencement of Act; the "Appointed Day"	102
THE ACT with Notes	105

PART I.

PARISH MEETINGS AND PARISH COUNCILS.

Constitution of Parish Meetings and Parish Councils.

SECTION
1. Constitution of Parish Meetings and establishment of Parish Councils 105

SECTION	PAGE
2. Parish Meetings	107
3. Constitution of Parish Council	108
4. Use of schoolroom	110

Powers and Duties of Parish Councils and Parish Meetings.

5. Parish Council to appoint Overseers	112
6. Transfer of certain powers of Vestry and other Authorities to Parish Council	113
7. Transfer of powers under Adoptive Acts	117
8. Additional powers of Parish Council	119
9. Powers for acquisition of land	122
10. Hiring of land for allotments	128
11. Restrictions on expenditure	132
12. Borrowing by Parish Council	133
13. Footpaths and roads	135
14. Public property and charities	136
15. Delegated powers of Parish Councils	139
16. Complaint by Parish Council of default of District Council	139
17. Parish officers and parish documents	140
18. Parish wards	143
19. Provisions as to small parishes	144

PART II.

Guardians and District Councils.

20. Election and qualification of Guardians	147
21. Names of County Districts and District Council	149
22. Chairman of Council to be Justice	150
23. Constitution of District Council in urban districts not being boroughs	150
24. Rural District Councils	152
25. Powers of District Council with respect to Sanitary and Highway matters	154
26. Duties and powers of District Council as to rights of way, rights of common, and roadside wastes	156

CONTENTS.

SECTION	PAGE
27. Transfer of powers of Justices to District Councils	158
28. Expenses of urban District Council	159
29. Expenses of rural District Council	159
30. Guardians in London and county boroughs	161
31. Provisions as to London vestries and District Boards	161
32. Application to county boroughs of provisions as to transfer of Justices' powers	162
33. Power to apply certain provisions of Act to urban districts and London	162
34. Supplemental provisions as to control of Overseers in urban districts	164
35. Restrictions on application of Act to London, &c.	164

PART III.

AREAS AND BOUNDARIES.

36. Duties and powers of County Council with respect to area and boundaries	165
37. Provision as to parishes having parts with defined boundaries	170
38. Orders for grouping parishes and dissolving groups	170
39. Provisions for increase and decrease of population	171
40. Certain orders of County Council not to require confirmation	172
41. Reduction of time for appealing against County Council orders	173
42. Validity of County Council orders	173

PART IV.

SUPPLEMENTAL.

Parish Meetings and Elections.

43. Removal of disqualification of married women	174
44. Register of parochial electors	174
45. Supplemental provisions as to Parish Meetings	177

CONTENTS.

SECTION	PAGE
46. Disqualifications for Parish or District Council	178
47. Supplemental provisions as to Parish Councils	181
48. Supplemental provisions as to elections, polls, and tenure of office	182
49. Provision as to Parish Meeting for part of parish	186
50. Supplemental provisions as to Overseers	187

Parish and District Councils.

51. Public notices	187
52. Supplemental provisions as to transfer of powers	188
53. Supplemental provisions as to Adoptive Acts	190
54. Effect on Parish Council of constitution of urban district	191
55. Power to change name of district or parish	193
56. Committees of Parish or District Councils	193
57. Joint Committees	195
58. Audit of Accounts of District and Parish Councils and Inspection	195
59. Supplemental provisions as to District Councils	197

Miscellaneous.

60. Supplemental provisions as to Guardians	198
61. Place of meeting of Parish or District Council or Board of Guardians	200
62. Permissive transfer to urban District Council of powers of other authorities	201
63. Provisions as to County Council acquiring powers of District Council	201
64. County Council may act through District Council	203
65. Saving for harbour powers	203
66. Saving for elementary schools	203
67. Transfer of property and debts and liabilities	204
68. Adjustment of property and liabilities	204
69. Power to deal with matters arising out of alteration of boundaries	206
70. Summary proceeding for determination of questions as to transfer of powers	207
71. Supplemental provisions as to County Council orders	208

CONTENTS.

SECTION	PAGE
72. Provisions as to local inquiries	208
73. Provision as to Sundays and bank holidays	209
74. Provisions as to Scilly Islands	209
75. Construction of Act	210
76. Extent of Act	213
77. Short Title	213

PART V.

Transitory Provisions.

78. First elections to Parish Councils	213
79. First elections of Guardians and District Councils	214
80. Power of County Council to remove difficulties	217
81. Existing officers	218
82. Provision as to highways	220
83. Duty of County Council to bring Act into operation	221
84. Appointed day	221
85. Current rates, &c.	224
86. Saving for existing securities and discharge of debts	225
87. Saving for existing byelaws	226
88. Saving for pending contracts, &c.	226
89. Repeal of Acts	226
First Schedule	229

APPENDIX (The Local Government Act, 1888 (ss. 54, 57, 58, 59, 120) 235

THE
LOCAL-GOVERNMENT ACT, 1894.

INTRODUCTION.

WHEN the third reading of the Local Government Bill of 1888 was agreed to in the House of Commons, MR. H. H. FOWLER described it as the first volume of a great work. The measure which he has himself with so much ability and success now piloted through Parliament, is the second volume of that work. It does, in fact, but complete the scheme commenced by the Bill of 1888, the object of which, as originally introduced, was not merely to confer on the counties a form of municipal government analogous to that possessed by boroughs, but to simplify the complicated areas of rating, and consolidate to some extent the numerous local authorities exercising powers within those areas. There was, it is true, no immediate intention on the part of the government then in power of extending local government to the villages, although, in introducing the Bill, Mr. C. T. RITCHIE stated that they would have been glad to propose a reconstruction of parochial organization, and that if they had not dealt with the question it was not because they did not recognise its importance, but because they felt the necessity of keeping their Bill within reasonable limits. County councils, however, having become part of our institutions, Parliament, in the Act which we are about to consider, has not only provided for the establishment of *district councils* (which formed part of the scheme of 1888, although that part of it was not proceeded with), but, with the view of revivifying the parish and giving to the rural electors a share in the administration of local affairs, it has made *parish councils* virtually an accomplished fact. Nor have the framers of the Act stopped here; but, wisely considering that a parochial council would be useless without a parochial opinion behind it, they give us the *parish meeting*,—an assembly in which all the electors of the parish (including women, married and single) have a right to take part, and which seems well-fitted to be the means of exciting such an interest in local affairs as it is the object of the Act to create.*

---

* The provisions of the Act as to boards of guardians and the London sanitary authorities are connected with those as to district councils, and will be dealt with in their proper place.

It would be interesting, before passing to the provisions of the Act, to trace the history of local government in England, and to show how our existing institutions have been arrived at; but this our space will not permit. As affecting the parish, however, it should be borne in mind that, great as are the changes now introduced, the Act does, in principle, but revive, with modifications suited to the present day, conditions such as existed at a very early period of our history, when in every township the freemen assembled in the township moot, under the presidency of the reeve, for the transaction of business and the discussion of their local affairs.

Those portions of the Act which deal with parish meetings and parish councils relate only to " rural parishes," that is, with parishes forming part of rural sanitary districts. A rural sanitary district is that part of a poor-law union which is not comprised in any urban sanitary district. The distinction is purely technical, for an " urban " district may contain a good deal of agricultural land, and a " rural " district may comprise areas of an urban or semi-urban character. If a parish is only partly in a rural sanitary district, the part which is within the district will be a rural parish for the purposes of the Act (s. 1).

In these "rural parishes," the parish meeting and parish council will between them, in November next, take over practically all the powers of the vestry meeting, except in so far as they have to do with the affairs of the Church or of ecclesiastical charities; and it will be convenient in the first place to indicate briefly the constitution of the vestry, and what its powers are at the present time. In this way the great changes to which we have alluded will best be made apparent.

The Vestry Meeting.*

Originally a meeting for ecclesiastical purposes of all the free inhabitants of the parish, the vestry afterwards became recognised as a meeting

---

* It will be understood that the remarks which follow apply to the general or open vestry. For the purposes of the Act no distinction is made between open and select vestries. (*See* s. 75.) The latter are not numerous, and it will be sufficient to observe with regard to them that they consist in each case of a limited number of vestrymen elected in some instances by custom, and elsewhere under Acts of Parliament, and that, subject to the provisions of any such Acts, a select vestry stands in the place of the general or open vestry, and possesses similar powers. It may be added that, for certain purposes, meetings of the inhabitants are held which are not strictly speaking vestry meetings; but as in the new Act the term "vestry" is used to include these (s. 75), it seems unnecessary to distinguish between such meetings and true vestries, for the purpose of the present work.

for the transaction of the general business of the parish, and this character it still retains. But its powers are somewhat shadowy, and as a gathering it distinctly lacks popularity. Speaking generally, every ratepayer of the parish, irrespective of sex, is entitled to be present and vote at a vestry meeting; but the number of the votes which may be given by any person depends upon the rateable value of the property for which he pays rates, the maximum number being six. The incumbent of the parish is *ex officio* chairman of the vestry. Its place of meeting is, of course, primarily the vestry of the parish church, or, where there is no vestry room attached to the church, the church itself. But in parishes with more than 2,000 inhabitants another meeting-place may be provided.

In addition to a general right of meeting for the discussion of matters affecting the parish, the powers and duties of the vestry include the following:—

(1.) It elects some of the parish officers.

> It does not appoint the *overseers*, although it is very usual for it to nominate persons from among whom the justices may select those whom they will appoint. The *churchwardens*, who are, in most cases, ex-officio overseers of the poor, are elected (in the absence of any special custom to the contrary) by the minister and parishioners in vestry, but if they cannot agree upon the choice of wardens, the minister chooses one and the parishioners another. The vestry may elect an *assistant overseer*, but he is appointed by warrant of

two justices. *Surveyors of highways* and *waywardens* are appointed by the vestry. In a parish of over 2,000 inhabitants, the Local Government Board may authorise the vestry to elect a *vestry clerk*.

(2.) The vestry have powers under the Lighting and Watching Act, 1833, the Baths and Washhouses Acts, the Burial Acts, the Public Improvement Act, 1860, and the Public Libraries Act, 1892.

> These Acts are in future to be known in relation to a parish as the "Adoptive Acts." They are not in force in any parish in which they have not been adopted, and in each case, except that of the Public Libraries Act (for which a different procedure is prescribed), the vestry at present have the power of adopting the Acts, although, as a matter of fact, the Acts (except the Lighting and Watching and Burial Acts), have to all intents and purposes remained thus far a dead letter as regards rural parishes. The Lighting and Watching Act has hitherto been carried into execution in a parish by *inspectors* appointed by the vestry, and the Baths and Washhouses Acts, the Public Improvement Act, and the Public Libraries Act would, after adoption, be executed by *commissioners* appointed by the vestry. For the purposes of the Burial Acts, a *burial board* is elected. Other matters connected with the Adoptive Acts are under the control of the vestry.

(3.) The vestry exercises some supervision in the matter of parish charities.

> For instance, the Charitable Trusts Act, 1855 (18 & 19 Vict. c. 124, s. 44), requires the trustees of parochial charities to make up their accounts annually, and to deliver a copy to the churchwardens, to be by them presented to the vestry and entered on its minutes. Under local schemes, the vestry may appoint trustees or beneficiaries of charities.

(4.) The vestry has some miscellaneous powers

as to highways, the management of allotments, the compounding (voluntary or compulsory) of owners for rates, the expenses of making valuation lists, the county rate basis, the provision of vestry rooms and parish offices, and the safe keeping of parish books and documents.

Other matters in which the vestry is more or less concerned might be mentioned, but enough has been said to indicate the character of the business at present transacted at vestry meetings, and to enable us, as we proceed, to bring into contrast the much fuller powers entrusted to the parochial bodies established by the new Act. What has been wanted is some means of popularising parish business—of interesting the parish in its own concerns; and the Act seeks to do this by constituting these new bodies—the one popular and the other popularly elected—to take over nearly all the civil business hitherto transacted by the vestry, with such added powers as should create an adequate field for the energy and intelligence of the parish, and conduce generally to a better administration in matters affecting its common life, prosperity and health.

We now propose to describe the constitution of the parish meeting, and the powers which are conferred upon it by the Act. We shall deal first with the case of all parishes for which separate parish councils will be elected, and afterwards with those treated exceptionally in this respect.

Parish Meetings.

Every rural parish, as described at page 15, will have its parish meeting, and in some cases parish meetings can be held for parts of parishes (ss. 1, 7, 18, 37, &c.). The persons who are entitled to attend and vote at the parish meeting are termed in the Act "parochial electors," and the term is explained in section 2 as meaning "the persons registered in such portion either of the local government register of electors, or of the parliamentary register of electors as relates to the parish." Where a parish meeting can be held for part of a parish, the parochial electors in that part only will have the right to attend (s. 49). The parochial electors constitute the electorate for all the elections under Mr. Fowler's Act, viz., elections of

- (*a*) parish councillors;
- (*b*) guardians;
- (*c*) district councillors;
- (*d*) metropolitan vestrymen and auditors, and members of the Woolwich Local Board.

It will be convenient, therefore, to deal with the whole question of the qualification of this new electorate before proceeding further.

Qualification of Parochial Electors.

The various qualifications may be thus stated:—

In counties the parliamentary register consists of males who, being of full age, are either

(1) owners of freeholds of the clear annual value of 40s. and upwards;
(2) tenants of copyholds of £5 annual value and upwards;
(3) leaseholders for twenty years and upwards of £50, or for sixty years of £5 annual value;
(4) occupiers of land or of tenements of the clear annual value of £10;
(5) lodgers who occupy lodgings which, if let unfurnished, are of the clear annual value of £10;
(6) occupiers of dwelling-houses without respect to value. (The occupiers of rooms in a house without a resident landlord are registered as occupiers.)
(7) occupiers of dwelling-houses belonging to their employers, as part of their service and without payment of rent.

In boroughs, with very few exceptions (the exceptions being cities which are counties of themselves), the parliamentary register contains neither freehold, copyhold, nor long leasehold voters. Owners whose qualifications arise within a parliamentary borough vote for the county at elections of members of parliament. S. 44 (2) of the new Act, however, provides for registered owners of property in a parliamentary borough voting as parochial electors for the parish in the borough within which their qualification arises.

The local government register, in addition to the qualifications above mentioned, numbered (4) and (6), contains a list of persons, both male and female, who occupy any house, warehouse, counting-house, shop, or other building within the county without respect to value, and who are resident within the county or within fifteen miles of its boundary (or, in the case of a municipal borough, in or within seven miles of the borough).

Married women otherwise qualified to be included in the local government register will, by virtue of section 43 of the new Act, be entitled to be put on that register "for the purposes of this Act." Husband and wife, however, cannot both be qualified in respect of the same property, *i.e.*, they cannot claim to be registered as joint occupiers. Either may be put on the register, but not both. The practical effect as regards a married woman seems to be that, supposing her to possess a qualification which, if she were single, would previously have entitled her to be put on the local government register, she can now claim to be put on a separate list of parochial electors which is to be prepared under section 44, and she can vote as parochial elector at a parish meeting, and in each of the elections above mentioned. No women owners, lodgers, or service franchise voters are introduced, because these qualifications belong only to the parliamentary register, which does not include women at all. It is only the local government register which is affected by section 43, and that is made up exclusively of occupation voters. A married woman will not apparently be able to vote in the election of town or county councillors, or members of a school board, as in neither of these cases is the election one of "the purposes of this Act." The Act in this respect has removed some anomalies only to create others. It is but right, however, to add that the forms of the House of Commons were held to preclude the insertion in this Bill of a clause conferring on married women the right to vote in the election of all local bodies, and we may expect that the municipal and school board franchise will very shortly be extended to married women by a separate measure.

A new electoral register, called the "register of the parochial electors," is to be formed, comprising all persons whose names are on either of the registers above described (including the separate list referred to), and every man and woman whose name is on the parochial register, and no others, will be entitled to attend a parish meeting and vote as a parochial elector, unless otherwise disqualified by law.*

The same person may be registered, if duly qualified, in more than one register of parochial electors, and may vote as a parochial elector in each parish for which he is registered. He will

* Persons guilty of corrupt or illegal practices at elections would be disqualified.

not, however, in any case, have more than one vote for the same parish.

Chairman, Place and Time of Meeting.

When present, the chairman of the parish council will be entitled to take the chair at the parish meeting, unless he is a candidate in an election which is to take place at the meeting. Should he be absent or be unable or unwilling to take the chair, the meeting will elect a chairman. In any case the occupant of the chair will have a casting vote (ss. 2, 45 and Sched. I, Part I).

The Act requires that a parish meeting shall be held every year on the 25th March, or within seven days before or after that date. The proceedings must in no case commence before six o'clock in the evening. Subject to this, the parish council will fix the times and places of meeting (ss. 2, 45 and Sched. I, Part I).

If there is in the parish no suitable public room vested in the parish council which can be used free of charge for a parish meeting, section 4 gives the parochial electors the right, subject to certain conditions, to use for this purpose any suitable room in a school receiving a parliamentary grant, or any other suitable room maintained at the cost of the rates. No charge is to be made for the use of the room; but any expense to which the managers may be put through such use, and the cost of making good any damage that may be done to the premises or to the furniture of the room in connection with the meeting, are to be defrayed, in the manner stated below, as part of the expenses of the meeting. The Act enables the parish council to provide a room for parish meetings; but among other rooms which would come within the terms of section 4, we might instance, besides board and voluntary schoolrooms, the board room or offices of the guardians, school board or other like authority. The section would also apply to a room used for the administration of justice or police. No parish meeting is to be held at an inn if there is any other suitable place available, either free of charge or at a reasonable cost (s. 61).

How Parish Meetings may be convened.

Parish meetings are to be convened by posting, not less than seven clear days before the date of the meeting, notices specifying the business to be transacted, at the doors of all the churches and chapels, and elsewhere in some conspicuous place in the parish, and, in addition, in any other manner that may be desirable. If it is proposed to adopt any of the Adoptive Acts, fourteen (instead of seven) days' notice of the meeting is necessary (s. 51, Sched. I, Part I). The first parish meeting will probably be held about the end of Nevember, 1894. It will be convened by the overseers. Subsequent meetings may be convened by the chairman, or any two members of the parish council, or any six parochial electors (ss. 45, 49, 78).

Voting, &c. at Parish Meeting; Polls.

At any parish meeting, or at a poll consequent thereon, no person may give more than one vote, except in the case of an election, when one vote may be given to each of any number of persons not exceeding the number to be elected. Questions before the meeting will be decided in the first instance by show of hands. A poll may be demanded at any time before the close of a meeting on any question which has been brought before it (including the election of parish councillors), and, if this is done, the poll must be taken by ballot. On certain specified subjects, any one parochial elector can demand a poll; but in other cases the chairman can refuse a poll unless the demand is made by at least five electors or by one-third of those present, whichever number is least. The parish council may make standing orders to regulate the proceedings and business at parish meetings, and the Local Government Board will issue rules for the conduct of polls (ss. 2, 48; Sched. I, Parts I, III).

Powers of the Parish Meeting.

As regards the powers which the Act confers on the parish meeting, it may be mentioned, first, that the electors have a general power to discuss the affairs of the parish and to pass resolutions thereon (Sched. I, Part I). In addition, the parish meeting will have the all-important power of electing the parish council, and within certain limits of controlling the expenditure of that body (ss. 11, 48); it will adopt any of the Adoptive Acts which it may be determined to put in force in the parish, and where, in any matters connected with those Acts, it has hitherto been necessary to obtain the consent or approval of the vestry, the consent or approval of the parish meeting will be required instead (s. 7).* Its consent will be necessary to the sale or exchange of any land or buildings which the Act vests in the parish council (s. 8). It can prevent the stopping or diversion of any public right of way, or the discontinuance of any highway which it is proposed to declare unnecessary (s. 13); it may consent to the letting, sale or exchange of workhouses, &c., or the application of the proceeds of the sale of such property; it can also give consent to the grant of parish land under the School Sites Acts as a site for a school, or under the Literary and Scientific Institutions Act, 1854 (17 & 18 Vict. c. 112), as a site for an institution for the promotion of science, literature, the fine arts, &c., and it is empowered to apply to the Education Department for the formation or dissolution of a school board (s. 52).

* A summary of the provisions of the Adoptive Acts will be found at page 42 *post*.

Expenses of Parish Meetings.

The expenses of parish meetings (including the expenses of polls) are to be paid by the parish council, who will obtain the sums required for the purpose by precepts on the overseers. The precepts will be met out of the poor rate (s. 11).

Parish Meetings treated exceptionally.

Where there is no separate parish council, the Act treats the parish meeting in an exceptional manner. In order to avoid repetition, we propose to deal with these cases after we have shown what powers are entrusted generally to parish councils. But first we have to consider how these councils are constituted.

Parish Councils.

A parish council will not, as a rule, be established for a parish with less than 300 inhabitants, although the Act provides machinery for the constitution of councils for smaller parishes, to which reference will be made in due course.*
It should also be stated that in the case of a rural parish which is co-extensive with a rural sanitary district, the district council will act as a parish council, and there will be no separate parish council unless directions to the contrary are given by the county council. But, with these exceptions,

* See page 56 *post.*

unless the parish consents to being "grouped," as afterwards described,* with another parish or parishes under a common parish council, there will be a separate parish council for every rural parish. The council will consist of a chairman and from five to fifteen councillors, as may be determined by the county council. It will be a body corporate, but will not have a common seal (ss. 1, 3, 36). Large parishes may be divided into wards for the election of councillors (s. 18).

Chairman and Vice-Chairman of Parish Council.

The chairman may be any person qualified to be a parish councillor, whether a member of the council or otherwise. He will be elected each year at the annual meeting of the council, which is to be held in April. The council may elect a vice-chairman, who must be a member of the council (s. 3; Sched. I, Part II).

Who may be Parish Councillors.

The council is to be elected from among the parochial electors of the parish, or persons who have for the twelve months preceding the election resided in the parish or within three miles of it. Women, whether married or single, may be elected if they possess either of these qualifications (s. 3).

* See page 57 *post.*

Election and Term of Office of Parish Councillors.

For the purpose of the election of parish councillors, a parish meeting must be convened. At this meeting, opportunity must be given for putting questions to any of the candidates who may be present, and for receiving explanations from them. Any candidate, whether a parochial elector, or not, is entitled to attend and speak at the meeting, although, of course, if he is not an elector he cannot vote. Rules for the conduct of the election (including the poll, if any) are to be framed by the Local Government Board (ss. 3, 48; Sched. I, Part I).* The first election of parish councillors will probably take place about the end of November, 1894.† At the first meeting after election, unless the council permit him to defer doing so to a later meeting, every councillor must sign, in the presence of some member of the council, a declaration that he accepts the office, but somewhat curiously the same requirement does not seem to apply in the case of the chairman, if he is elected from outside.‡

Any casual vacancy occurring on the council will be filled by them at a meeting convened for

---

* *See* page 90 *post.*

† *See* page 102 *post.*

‡ *Cf* rule (1) of Sched. I, Part II, which applies only to "parish councillors."

the purpose (s. 47; Sched. I, Part II). The term of office of parish councillors will usually be one year from the 15th April, but the first councillors will be in office from November, 1894, till April 1896 (ss. 3, 78).

Officers of the Parish Council.

The parish council may appoint a clerk and treasurer. The former officer, if unpaid, may be one of the parish councillors. If a councillor is not appointed, the assistant overseer, or one of the assistant overseers, will be the clerk. Where there is no assistant overseer the Act provides for the appointment of a collector of poor rates, or some other fit person, as clerk. The parish council are not to make any appointment to the office of vestry clerk, but if the parish has already a vestry clerk, he is to be the first clerk of the council. The treasurer may be any person selected by the parish council, whether a member of the council or not. He cannot be paid for his services. If the council act as a parochial committee under a provision referred to below, they will have the assistance of the clerk of the district council (ss. 17, 81).

Meetings of Parish Council.

A parish council are required to hold at least four meetings a year. One of these is the annual meeting. Unless the council expressly direct otherwise, all their meetings will be open to the public, but they are not bound, like the parish meeting, to assemble at any particular time in the day. In order to convene a meeting three clear days' notice must be given in writing to every member of the council stating the time and place of meeting and the business to be transacted. In the case of the annual meeting, notice specifying these particulars must be given to every member of the council immediately after his election. The person to convene a meeting is primarily the chairman of the council. If, however, two councillors present a requisition, and the chairman thereupon refuses or neglects to convene a meeting, any two members of the council may convene it (Scbed. I, Part II). The first meeting of the parish council should be convened by the chairman of the parish meeting at which the first councillors are nominated (s. 78).

As to the place of meeting, it will be seen, when we come to deal with the powers of the council, that they can provide suitable rooms for meetings, offices, &c. But, like the parish meeting and on like conditions, they will be empowered (*see* s. 4) to use the schoolroom or any suitable room which is maintained at the cost of the rates. Mention has been made at page 25 of some of the rooms to which this remark applies. It may be added that in a civil parish which is co-extensive with an ecclesiastical parish, and in which the Vestries Act, 1850, has not been put in force, there would seem to be no legal obstacle to the parish council holding their meetings in the vestry of the parish church, or, if there is no vestry, in the church itself;* but there are obvious reasons why another place should be selected if possible. Meetings at an inn are only permitted by the Act in cases where no suitable room elsewhere is available free of charge or at a reasonable cost (s. 61).

Voting, &c., at Meetings of Parish Council.

Every question before the council is to be decided by the votes of the majority of those present and voting on the question, and to constitute a quorum at least one-third, and in any case not less than three of the members must be present. The chairman has a casting vote. The council may make standing orders as to their proceedings. Minutes must be kept, and the names of the members present at any meeting are to be recorded, and also, in the case of a division, the names of those voting and how they voted (Sched. I, Parts II, III).

Powers of the Parish Council.

Sections 5 to 16 deal with some of the principal powers which are given to parish councils. The space at command prevents our attempting more

---

* Sec. 6 transfers to the parish council nearly all the "powers" of the vestry. "Powers" includes "rights" (Local Government Act, 1888, sec. 100, and sec. 75 of the present Act).

than a summary of these provisions; and for fuller details we must refer our readers to the Act itself.

Under section 5 the council will appoint—not merely nominate for appointment by justices—the overseers, and also assistant overseers. The churchwardens will cease to be overseers, but an additional number of overseers may be appointed to fill their place. Overseers should be "substantial householders" (43 Eliz. c. 2), and should be appointed at the annual meeting of the parish council immediately after the election of the chairman (s. 5; Sched. I, Part II). Women may be appointed as overseers. "Any discreet person" (including a woman) may be assistant overseer (59 Geo. III, c. 12, s. 7). When the parish council have appointed the overseers for the year they must give notice of the appointment to the guardians. The possible failure to make the appointment at the proper time is provided for by section 50.

Section 5 also vests in the parish council the legal interest in lands or other property (unconnected with the church or with ecclesiastical charities*) now vested either in the overseers, or in the churchwardens and overseers. This provision will be referred to again under the heading of public property and charities.†

Section 6 transfers to the parish council all the

---

* See the definition of "ecclesiastical charity" in section 75.
† See page 48 *post*.

powers, duties, and liabilities of the vestry,* except those relating to the affairs of the church or ecclesiastical charities, those which the Act transfers from the vestry to the parish meeting, and those relating to highways, which are transferred to the district council.† The vestry, therefore, in a rural parish, will revert practically to its original status as a meeting for ecclesiastical purposes only.

The powers of the churchwardens are similarly dealt with. They are relieved of all civil functions, and will retain only their jurisdiction in affairs of the church and ecclesiastical charities. They will, however, no longer be responsible for maintaining closed churchyards where the expenses fall upon the poor rate under the Burial Act, 1855 (18 & 19 Vict. c. 128).

Section 18 of the Act referred to provides that where a churchyard is closed for burials by an Order in Council, the churchwardens shall maintain the churchyard in decent order, and do the necessary repair of the walls and other fences. The churchwardens' expenses in the matter are to be repaid by the overseers " upon the certificate of the churchwardens," out of the poor rate, " unless

---

* As to the powers of the vestry, see pages 17 to 19 *ante.*

† See, however, s. 25. If the operation of that section is postponed, as therein mentioned, the parish council will in the meanwhile exercise the powers of the vestry under the Highway Acts.

there shall be some other fund legally chargeable" with the expenses. Where, under this enactment, the expenses fall on any fund other than the poor rate, the churchwardens will retain control of the churchyard, and even where the cost has hitherto fallen on the poor rate, the churchwardens will not lose the control of the churchyard if no further demand is made by them for the repayment of any expenses out of that rate.

Section 6 of the Local Government Act, 1894, also transfers to the parish council the powers and duties possessed by the overseers, either alone or in conjunction with the churchwardens, in relation to the following matters, viz.:

- (i.) appeals or objections by them in respect of the valuation list, or appeals in respect of the poor rate, or county rate, or the basis of the county rate; and
- (ii.) the provision of parish books and of a vestry room or parochial office, parish chest, fire-engine, fire escape, or matters relating thereto; and
- (iii.) the holding or management of parish property, not being property relating to affairs of the church or held for an ecclesiastical charity, and the holding or management of village greens, or of allotments, whether for recreation grounds or for gardens or otherwise for the benefit of the inhabitants or any of them.

Paragraph (i.) will enable the council to defend the interests of the parish in matters relating to the assessment of property. A vestry room or parochial office can be provided under paragraph (ii.) if the population of the parish justifies such provision, and a parish fire-engine if there is no other authority competent to provide one.

Under paragraph (iii.), read in connection with subsection (4), which transfers to the parish council the powers and duties of allotment wardens and others, the council will be empowered to prevent encroachments on village greens, and will take under their control any fuel allotments or allotments for field gardens, and recreation grounds under the Inclosure Acts. The mention of these matters suggests topics of considerable interest in connection with the growth of the allotment system; but at the present time far greater practical importance attaches to the arrangements for the acquisition of land under the Allotments Acts, 1887 and 1890, as amended by Mr. Fowler's Act. This branch of the subject will be dealt with under a separate heading.*

The principal matters left in the hands of the overseers after the transfer of the powers above mentioned will be,—

    (*a*) the making, and the responsibility for the collection of the poor rate and other rates;
    (*b*) the discharge of orders for contributions to the union, &c., that have to be met out of those rates;
    (*c*) the making out of jury lists; and
    (*d*) the preparation of lists of voters.

* *See* page 45 *post*.

Such powers as they now possess in regard to the relief of the poor (these being confined to cases of sudden and urgent necessity), the bringing before justices and conveyance to asylums of lunatics, the burial of drowned persons cast up by the sea or navigable rivers, the making out of new valuation lists, and some other powers are also reserved to them.

Section 6 further transfers to the parish council certain powers with regard to the letting, sale, or exchange of parish property, which are now exercised by the guardians under the control of the Local Government Board.

The same section enables the parish council to make complaints or representations under sections 31 and 38 of the Housing of the Working Classes Act, 1890, with a view to the closing or demolition of buildings which are either themselves unfit for habitation, or by their situation or otherwise tend to make other buildings unhealthy, or to prevent proper measures being taken with regard to unhealthy dwellings. How necessary such powers as these may be in some rural places can hardly be appreciated by dwellers in towns.

It has been shown that the parish meeting has the power of adopting the "Adoptive Acts." Sections 7 and 53 make the parish council the authority for putting these Acts into execution in all cases where the Acts are adopted in a rural parish after the present Act comes into force.

They also transfer to the council the execution of any of the Adoptive Acts that may already have been adopted in a rural parish, except where they are at present in force in part only of the parish; and in that case the powers of the inspectors, commissioners, or board now administering the Act *may* be transferred to the council.*

Section 8 gives the parish council the following additional powers. They may provide buildings for offices, meetings and other public purposes. They may acquire and lay out recreation grounds and public walks, and may regulate by means of byelaws any recreation ground, village green, or other open space under their control, or may close any of these to the public for a limited number of days in the year, and grant the use of it on those days for certain objects, either gratuitously or for payment. Provided they do not interfere with any public or private rights, the council may utilise wells and springs in the parish, and give facilities to the inhabitants for obtaining water therefrom. They may drain or cleanse foul ditches and stagnant pools, and deal with accumulations of refuse which are likely to be prejudicial to health. The giving of these powers to the parish council makes it none the less the duty of the district council to provide a water supply and undertake sanitary works; but cases will frequently arise in

* A summary of the provisions of the Adoptive Acts will be found at page 42.

which very useful work of the kind referred to can be undertaken by the parish council, without interfering with the general powers of the district council. The parish council may acquire (but not compulsorily) rights of way, if this would be beneficial to the parish; and gifts of property may be accepted and held by them for the benefit of the parish. Lands or buildings vested in the council may be let, sold, or exchanged by them, subject to proper conditions. The Board of Agriculture may be called upon by them to issue information and direction as to the mode in which applications are to be made for provisional orders for the regulation or inclosure of commons.* Notice of any such application must be served upon the council.

Section 13 provides that, for the future, a public right of way shall not be stopped or diverted, or a highway be discontinued as unnecessary† without the consent of the parish council. The consent, however, if given, may be vetoed by the parish meeting. The council may, under the same section, undertake the repair of public footpaths in the parish.

Under section 202 of the Public Health Act, 1875, a " parochial committee," consisting wholly

---

* For powers as to commons conferred on district councils, see page 79 *post*.

† *See* 5 and 6 Will. IV, c. 50, ss. 84 to 91; 41 & 42 Vict. c. 77, s. 24.

or partly of members of a rural sanitary authority, may be appointed by that authority, to exercise within a parish such powers as the authority could exercise therein. Under section 15 of the present Act, if a parochial committee, consisting only in part of members of the district council are appointed, the other members must be members of the parish council; but powers may be delegated to the parish council by the district council as though the former were a parochial committee.

Under section 16, if the district council adopt any scheme of sewerage or water supply affecting the parish, the parish council must have notice before the contract is given out. This section also enables the parish council to complain to the county council of any failure on the part of the district council to perform their duties in respect of the parish, especially in the matter of sewerage or water supply or the maintenance of highways. The effect of such a complaint, if justified, would be to enable the county council to take upon themselves the powers of the district council in the matter and execute the necessary works; or, if they preferred, the county council would be empowered to make an order for the performance of the neglected duty by the district council within a specified time, and if it was not performed within that time, they could appoint a person to carry out the works. In either case their expenses would be recoverable from the district council.

The Adoptive Acts.

The principal provisions of the Adoptive Acts affecting rural parishes are as follows:—

The Lighting and Watching Act, 1833 (3 & 4 Will. IV, c. 90), provides for the lighting of streets in parishes, and parts of parishes, the provision of fire-engines, &c. It may be adopted either in whole or in part. It requires a two-thirds majority of those voting to adopt the Act. If it is adopted, the parish meeting must fix the amount to be levied for the purposes of the Act. The sum fixed is raised by means of a separate rate, to which occupiers of land are assessed in the proportion of one-third only of the rate in the pound paid by the occupiers of houses, buildings and property, other than land.

The Baths and Washhouses Acts, 1846 to 1882,* may also be adopted by a two-thirds majority of those voting, subject, however, to the approval of the Local Government Board. The Acts authorise the appropriation of parish lands, or the purchase or taking on lease of land, and the erection thereon of baths and washhouses, or the purchase or taking on lease of existing baths and washhouses. They also authorise the provision of swimming baths and open bathing places. During winter any swimming bath established under the

---

* 9 & 10 Vict. c. 74; 10 & 11 Vict. c. 61; 41 & 42 Vict. c. 14; 45 & 46 Vict. c. 30.

Acts may be used as a gymnasium, &c. At any time, when not required for the purposes of the Acts, any public baths may be used for vestry meetings, or other parochial purposes. Neighbouring parishes may concur in providing baths and washhouses. The expenses of carrying the Acts into execution, to such amount as the parish meeting may sanction, are payable out of the poor rate. The Acts confer borrowing powers, which will be exerciseable by the parish council.

The Burial Acts, 1852 to 1885, relate to the provision of burial grounds and mortuaries. A parish meeting may be convened to determine whether a burial ground shall be provided for the parish, and the question must be taken into consideration if it is proposed to close the churchyard on the ground that it is crowded or insanitary. A resolution in favour of providing a burial ground will constitute an adoption of the Burial Acts for the purposes of the new Local Government Act (s. 7). The Acts authorise the appropriation of parish or charity land, or the purchase of land for a cemetery, or a contract may be entered into with another body or authority having a cemetery for the interment of parishioners therein. Two or more parishes may also "concur" in providing a common cemetery. The expenses of carrying the Acts into execution are paid out of the poor rate. The cost of providing and laying out the burial ground and building the necessary chapels may be met by a loan on the security of the poor rate. It must not, however, exceed a sum fixed by the parish meeting.

The Public Improvements Act, 1860 (23 & 24 Vict. c. 30), only applies to parishes with a population exceeding 500 persons. This, too, may be adopted by a two-thirds majority of the persons voting. It enables the parish to acquire land, and accept gifts of land for the purpose of forming or improving public walks, and exercise or play-grounds. When one-half the estimated cost of the improvement has been raised by private subscription or donation, a separate rate of not more than 6d. in the pound may be imposed by a two-thirds majority of the parish meeting.*

The Public Libraries Act, 1892 (55 & 56 Vict. c. 53), may be adopted by means of a poll of the parochial electors. It cannot be adopted without a poll.† The rate for library purposes must not exceed one penny in the pound in any one year, but it may be limited to one halfpenny or threefarthings in the pound, as the case may be. The Act enables the parish to provide for itself not only public libraries, but also public museums, schools for science, art galleries, and

---

* The provision that it shall be a two-thirds majority "in value" is repealed by the present Act.

† *See* section 3 of the Act of 1892, and section 7 of the Local Government Act, 1894.

schools for art. Two or more parishes. may combine for library purposes, or a parish may be annexed for those purposes to an adjoining district. The expenses of executing the Act, to such amount as is sanctioned by the parish meeting, will be paid out of a rate levied with and as part of the poor rate, with an allowance of two-thirds of the amount to occupiers of certain lands. The Act confers borrowing powers.

Acquisition of Land for Allotments, etc.

Clauses 9 and 10, which relate to the acquisition of land for allotments and other purposes, may very well be described as an Act in themselves. They comprise no fewer than thirty subsections, and apply by reference the Lands Clauses Acts, and numerous provisions in the Public Health Act, 1875, the Allotments Acts, 1887 and 1890, and other Acts. Under the Act of 1887 the sanitary authority are empowered by purchase, or hire, to acquire land for allotments, either on their own initiative or on the representation of six parliamentary electors or ratepayers. If compulsory powers are needed, a provisional order has to be obtained from the county council, which requires confirmation by Parliament. Under the Act of 1890, if a representation is made to a sanitary authority, but no action is taken by them, there is an appeal to the county council. There is no appeal under either of these Acts from the decision of the county council. The present Act, by doing away with the provisional order system, greatly cheapens and facilitates the acquisition of land for allotments. Under s. 9, if allotments are required, the parish council (*see* s. 6), or six parliamentary electors, may apply to the district council, who may provide the allotments. If the district council do not move in the matter, or if they require compulsory powers, the county council may make an order, which now only requires confirmation by the Local Government Board. There is an appeal to that Department if the county council refuse to make an order. Where the order is made and is found to be in accordance with the Act and regulations which the Local Government Board will prescribe, it will, as a matter of course, be confirmed, unless a memorial is presented to the Board praying for further inquiry. Where such a memorial is presented the Local Government Board will hold an inquiry in the locality, after which they may confirm or disallow the order as they think proper. The Lands Clauses Acts are to be incorporated in any order for the compulsory purchase of land under this section, but questions of disputed compensation are to be referred to a single arbitrator. At any inquiry or arbitration under this clause neither counsel nor expert witnesses are to be heard, except in cases prescribed by the Local Government Board; and in awarding compensation the arbitrator is not to make any additional allowance in respect of the purchase being compulsory.

Under the Acts of 1887 and 1890 there is no power for the compulsory *hiring* of land for allotments. Section 10 of the Act of this year gives power to the parish council to hire land for this purpose, and if they cannot do so by agreement they can appeal to the county council, who can make an order applying the Lands Clauses Acts, and authorising compulsory hiring for not less than fourteen nor more than thirty-five years. This order is subject to the same provisions as to confirmation by the Local Government Board as an order under section 9. The procedure therefore is both cheap and expeditious. No parliamentary costs are incurred, and, it may be added, no additional rent is to be paid for the land in respect of the hiring being compulsory. Disputed points can be referred to a single arbitrator. Where the council hire land for allotments, they may let to one person more than one acre (which is the limit under the Act of 1887); but if the hiring is compulsory, not more than one acre of arable land, and not more in the whole than four acres, can be let to the same person. No permanent pasture may be broken up without the written assent of the landlord.

The same easy method of compulsory purchase as is applicable for the provision of allotments, *i.e.*, by an order of the county council confirmed by the Local Government Board, can be applied for the purposes of baths, libraries, or any other matter in connection with which the parish council are authorised to acquire land, if they are unable to obtain suitable land by agreement on reasonable terms (s. 9).

Public Property and Charities.

With the exception of the clauses relating to the acquisition of land for allotments, no portions of the measure were more strongly contested in both Houses of Parliament than those which deal with public property and charities. It would be wholly out of place in this volume to discuss the merits of a question which must of necessity be approached by different parties from entirely opposite standpoints. We are now only concerned with the effect of the Act. And the first point to be noted is that, as Mr. Fowler has more than once contended, the Act draws "a broad dividing line between civil and ecclesiastical matters." Unfortunately, this at once suggests the question—What are matters ecclesiastical? And speaking broadly, this has been the real question at issue. The Act itself, however, must be taken as settling the matter, especially in relation to charities. By section 75 it defines what are " ecclesiastical charities," and if the definition is not such as to satisfy all parties, it certainly removes some of the original objections raised to the Bill. Thus, while "dole charities" are treated as non-ecclesiastical, except where they are for the benefit of members of any particular church or denomination, no "mission room" will be within the purview of the Act, and "parish rooms" also will be exempt if "in the opinion of the Charity Commissioners" they have been erected within the last forty years mainly by or at the cost of members of a particular church or denomination. Nothing in the Act (*see* s. 66) is to affect the trusteeship or management of elementary schools.

The only other provisions to which it seems necessary to call attention are those contained in sections 5, 6, and 14. The first of these sections, as previously observed,* will vest in the parish council the legal interest in property now vested in the overseers or the churchwardens and overseers of any rural parish; but this is intended† to deal "simply and exclusively with the legal ownership of property,—what lawyers would call bare trusteeship." It expressly provides that the property shall vest in the council subject to all trusts and liabilities affecting the same, and it does not apply to property connected with the affairs of the church or an ecclesiastical charity, nor to any property held by the church-

* *See* page 34 *ante*.

† *See* Mr. Fowler's speech in the House of Commons, in moving the second reading of the Bill (2nd Nov., 1893).

wardens or overseers jointly with any other person, as, for example, the minister. Section 6, transferring to the council the powers and duties of churchwardens, excepts all matters pertaining to the church or charities, and does not affect them in their capacity of trustees, which is dealt with in section 14.* It is in the latter section naturally that the greatest interest centres. It enacts, in the first place, that the trustees of public recreation grounds, rooms for public meetings, allotments for the benefit of the inhabitants and the like (ecclesiastical charities being once more expressly excepted) *may*, with the approval of the Charity Commissioners, transfer the property to the parish council, or to persons appointed by the latter. The transfer is clearly not obligatory on the trustees, and the section provides that if the council accept the transfer, they or their appointees must hold the property subject to all the existing trusts. The one matter in which ecclesiastical, as well as other parochial charities, may be touched by this clause is the substitution under subsection (2) of trustees appointed by the parish council for the overseers, where the latter are trustees of a charity either alone or jointly with other persons. The subsection would dispossess neither the minister nor the churchwardens in the case of an ecclesiastical charity; but if the churchwardens,

* We again cite the very excellent speech of Mr. Fowler on this subject.

as churchwardens, were trustees of a non-ecclesiastical charity, the substitution would apply to them also. The next subsection applies to every parochial charity* other than an ecclesiastical charity, and provides that where the governing body does not include what is usually termed a "representative element," the parish council may appoint additional members of that body not exceeding the number allowed by the Charity Commissioners. In the case of a sole trustee the number of trustees may be increased to three, one of whom may be nominated by the sole trustee and one by the parish council. The trusts, however, will be unaffected. The clause provides for the appointment in certain cases of trustees or beneficiaries by the parish council, or their appointees, in lieu of the vestry. Trustees appointed by the parish council will hold office for four years, one half retiring every second year. But the power of the council to appoint trustees (except where it is merely a power transferred to them from the vestry) cannot in the case of a charity founded before the passing of the Act, wholly or partly by a now living donor, be exercised without his consent until the year 1934, and, in the case of any other charity, until the expiration of forty years from its foundation.

It may be added that section 70 provides for the

* As defined by section 75.

settlement of questions that may arise as to the appointment of trustees or beneficiaries of charities, or as to the persons in whom charity property is vested.

Committees of Parish Council.

The parish council may delegate almost any of their powers to committees consisting either solely of members of the council, or partly of members and partly of other persons. If the parish council have any powers or duties which are to be exercised in a part only of a parish, or in relation to property held by them for the benefit of a part of a parish, they can, if the part in question has a defined boundary, be required to exercise such powers and duties by a committee consisting partly of persons representing that part. A committee appointed by a parish council may meet either within or outside the parish as is most convenient, but both its proceedings and the place of meeting may be regulated by the council, and its acts will not be valid without their approval (s. 56 ; Scbed. I, Part IV). The parish council may concur in appointing joint committees for any purposes in which they and other councils are jointly interested (s. 57).

Expenditure of the Parish Council.

The expenses of the parish council (including the expenses of the parish meeting, which will be defrayed by the council) will be paid out of the poor rate, on precepts addressed by the council to the overseers.* The Act enables the parish council to levy for their expenses not more than sixpence in the pound in any one year. This amount must cover all their expenses, except expenses under any of the Adoptive Acts. They cannot incur an expenditure representing more than three pence in the pound for the year without the consent of the parish meeting, and no expenditure involving a loan can be incurred by them without the consent of the parish meeting and the approval of the county council. They will keep accounts in a form prescribed by the Local Government Board (ss. 11, 58).†

Borrowing Powers of Parish Council.

The consent and approval referred to in the last paragraph are required to enable the parish council to incur any expense to defray which a loan is contemplated. The actual borrowing (which may be postponed until the full amount of the contem-

* The overseers' demand notes for rates must show the amount required for the expenses of the parish council and the proportion, if any, levied for the purpose of any of the Adoptive Acts (s. 11).

† As to the audit of accounts, *see* page 99 *post.*

plated expenditure is ascertained) is subject in every case to the consent of the county council and the Local Government Board. The parish council are authorised to borrow money for purchasing land or erecting buildings; for any purpose for which they are empowered to borrow under the Adoptive Acts; and for any permanent work or other matter, the cost of which the county council and the Local Government Board assent to being spread over a term of years. They may borrow the amount required from the county council. Certain provisions of the Public Health Act, 1875, are, with some modification, made applicable where the parish council borrow money. The provisions in question, and the effect of them as applied to the parish council, are briefly as follows:—

Section 233. The parish council may borrow or re-borrow money necessary for any of the purposes for which they are authorised to borrow, or for discharging loans contracted for any such purpose, and, as security, may mortgage the poor rate and the revenues of the parish council.

Section 234. The exercise of the power of borrowing is subject to the following (among other) regulations:—

> (1.) The sum borrowed must not at any time exceed, with the balances of outstanding loans, one-half the assessable value of the premises assessable within the parish.
>
> (2.) The money may be borrowed for such time, not exceeding 60 years, as the Local Government Board may sanction.* The loan may be repaid either by

---

* The full term of 60 years is very seldom allowed. About 30 years is the time usually fixed.

annual instalments, or by means of a sinking fund properly invested.

(3.) Where money is borrowed to discharge a previous loan, the time for repayment is not to extend beyond the date fixed for the repayment of the original loan, except with the consent of the Local Government Board.

Section 236. [This relates to the form of mortgage.]

Section 237. A register of mortgages is to be kept and is to be open to inspection.

Section 238. A mortgage may be transferred, and a register of transfers is to be kept.

Section 239. A receiver may, in certain cases, be appointed by a court of summary jurisdiction, on the application of a mortgagee.

Where the parish council raise a loan for any purpose connected with the Adoptive Acts, the charges for repayment of principal and interest must fall ultimately on the rate which is applicable to the purpose of the particular Act or Acts in connection with which the loan is raised (s. 12).

Parish Books and Documents.

The custody of the registers of baptisms, marriages, and burials, and, speaking generally, all other books and documents containing entries relating to the affairs of the church or ecclesiastical charities, is not interfered with by the Act; but, under section 17, the parish council will be empowered to give directions as to the persons with whom, or the place in which, other books and papers belonging to the parish shall be deposited.

The county council are to make periodical inquiry as to the manner in which books and documents under the control of the parish council are kept, with a view to their proper preservation. Any documents now required by statute or the standing orders of Parliament to be deposited with the parish clerk, such as maps, plans, &c., of proposed railways and like undertakings, are, for the future, to be deposited with the clerk, or, where there is no clerk, the chairman of the parish council. The last of the civil functions of the parish clerk seems to be thus taken away in rural parishes.

Hitherto we have been considering the case of parishes with more than 300 inhabitants in which parish councils will be established compulsorily by the Act. We have now to deal with the smaller parishes, in which, if parish councils are established, it will be by means of the special machinery to which reference was made above.

Special Provisions as to Small Rural Parishes.

Although a rural parish with less than 300 inhabitants will not, as a matter of course, have any parish council, it will have a parish meeting constituted in the same way as in any larger parish. A parish council can, however, be established in any such parish by an order of the county council, with the consent or on the application of the parish meeting, and it is competent to the parish meeting, if the parish has not less than 100 inhabitants, to demand to have a parish council, and the county council must comply with such a demand (ss. 1, 38). It is understood that 6,356 rural parishes out of a total number of 13,235 have a population of less than 300; but the object is to avoid forcing a parish council on a parish which has very few electors, and while providing for the establishment of a council in any case where there may be a desire for one, to make the grant dependent in great measure on the circumstances of the parish.

If a parish council is established for any of these "small parishes," the Act will apply to the parish in the same way as if a parish council were created for it by the Act. It is unnecessary, therefore, to say more about a case of this description. But one of the original proposals of the Bill was that small parishes should be grouped together, and a parish council be established for the group. The Act goes further in this respect, and provides that, if the parish meeting consent, the county council may group any rural parish (whatever its population) with a neighbouring parish or parishes under a common parish council, but with a separate parish meeting (s. 1). As a rule all the grouped parishes must be within the same county and county district.* The "grouping order" must

---
* The term "county district" is defined by s. 21. It is equivalent to the more familiar expression "sanitary district."

provide (s. 38) for the holding of parish meetings in each of the grouped parishes, and for the election of separate representatives of each parish on the parish council, and it *may* make necessary the consent of the parish meeting to certain acts of the parish council, and in other ways adapt the provisions of the Act to the circumstances of the case. If there are any charities attached to either of the grouped parishes, the order must make such provision as regards the appointment of trustees and beneficiaries as will preserve the rights of the parish. The custody of parish documents must also be provided for. The parish meeting of any parish may themselves apply to the county council to have a grouping order made respecting it. A group of parishes, or the parish council for a separate parish, may, under certain circumstances, be dissolved, or a particular parish may be separated from a group, and if the county council think proper a parish council may be established for that parish (ss. 38, 39).

Parishes without Parish Councils.

In the case of every parish which has not a separate parish council, the effect of the Act will depend to a great extent on whether the parish is " grouped " or not. If it is grouped, many of the powers that would otherwise be vested in the parish meeting will be transferred to the parish council of the group. In the absence, however, of any grouping order affecting the parish, section 19 requires that the parish meeting shall assemble at least twice a year. The place of meeting may be the schoolroom, or any other room such as we have mentioned in connection with the parish meetings of parishes having councils.* In addition, where there is no parish council and the parish is co-extensive with the ecclesiastical parish, the parish meeting would seem to be entitled to meet at the parish church or in the vestry room attached thereto.

At the "annual assembly" of the parish meeting, which, as in other cases, is to take place on the 25th March, or within seven days before or after that date, the meeting is to choose a chairman for the year. Subject to the requirement that there shall be two meetings a year, and also to the provision in section 2 requiring all meetings to be held in the evening, the chairman thus chosen is to fix the dates and places of meeting during his term of office, and the meetings are as a rule to be convened by him, although any six parochial electors may convene a meeting (s. 45).

If the business to be transacted relates to a proposal to "group" the parish, or establish a parish council, or to adopt any of the Adoptive Acts, fourteen days' notice must be given. In other cases, only seven days' notice is requisite.

* *See* page 25 *ante.*

The provisions as to voting at parish meetings and the right to demand a poll are substantially the same in the cases now under consideration as in those where there are parish councils; but, as will be seen, much more important powers are given to the parish meeting if the parish has not a council, and consequently the matters in regard to which it is within the power of a single parochial elector to demand a poll are more numerous. A list of these matters is given in Part I of the First Schedule to the Act.

The powers of the parish meeting in these cases will include nearly all those now exerciseable by the vestry which do not relate to the affairs of the church or to ecclesiastical charities. Besides this, the parish meeting will appoint the overseers and the assistant overseer (if any). The chairman and the overseers will be a body corporate, with power to hold land, but are to act under the direction of the parish meeting. The legal interest in property which, if there were a parish council, would be vested in the latter by section 5, will in these parishes vest in the chairman and overseers. Where (*see* p. 50) the parish council (if any) would appoint trustees of a charity in the place of overseers or churchwardens, the parish meeting will make the appointments. The provisions of the Act as to stopping or diverting public rights of way, and discontinuing unnecessary highways, and with respect to complaints of default on the part of district councils (*see* pp. 40, 41, 79), are to apply to the parish meeting in these parishes; and the county council may confer on the parish meeting, on the application of the latter, any of the powers conferred on a parish council by the Act.

The parish meeting may appoint a committee for any purposes which, in the opinion of the meeting, would be better regulated and managed by means of such a committee. It is obvious that, in many cases where the parish is too small, or perhaps too poor, to make it desirable that it should have a parish council, the parochial electors will yet be too numerous for the convenient exercise of their powers on all occasions " in parish meeting assembled." The appointment of a committee, however, will constitute virtually a small executive body, whose acts, it is true, will require to be submitted to the parish meeting for approval, but whose existence may render it unnecessary to convene a parish meeting more frequently than, say, twice a year, *i.e.*, on the two occasions in each year on which a meeting has to be held to comply with the Act. The result will be very much the same as if the parish had a parish council, but with less expense.

The Act fixes sixpence in the pound as the maximum amount of rate leviable in any year for defraying the expenses of the parish meeting where there is no parish council; and it should be noticed that this sum is to include all expenses under the

Adoptive Acts. The chairman will obtain the amount required for the expenses of the meeting from the overseers out of the poor rate (s. 11).

If the population of a parish without a parish council increases so as to justify the election of one, the county council may issue an order making the necessary arrangements (s. 39).

The next branch of our subject relates to guardians of the poor.

Guardians.

The provisions affecting guardians are chiefly contained in section 20 of the Act. They apply to the whole of England and Wales, including the metropolis; and although they do not touch the general policy of the poor laws, they involve some sweeping changes in connection with—

(*a*) the constitution of boards of guardians;
(*b*) the qualification for election as guardian;
(*c*) the electors;
(*d*) the conduct of the election;
(*e*) the term of office of guardians,

and several other matters.

At present there are three classes of guardians— *ex-officio*, nominated, and elective. The *ex-officio* guardians are justices residing in the union and acting for the county in which any part of the union is situated. The nominated guardians are found only in London. They are nominees of the Local Government Board. The qualification for an elective guardian consists, under the general law, in being rated to the poor rate at not less than £5. The electors are the ratepayers and such owners of property in the union as have made a claim to vote. Non-resident owners may vote by proxy. There is plural voting by means of voting papers delivered and collected from door to door. The term of office of elective guardians is usually one year. In the case, however, of about one-sixth of the boards of guardians, it is three years. In these cases either one-third of the guardians retire every year or all retire together every third year, the latter arrangement being far the more common.

The general effect of the new Act with reference to guardians is as follows:—There will no longer be any *ex-officio* or nominated guardians, but the board of guardians may elect from outside their own body a chairman or vice-chairman, or both, and not more than two other persons qualified to be guardians, who, in the language of the Act, will be "additional guardians and members of the board." If they do so elect—it is not obligatory upon them to do so—and if on the first election there is a sufficient number of persons who have served as *ex-officio* or nominated guardians, those persons are to have preference in the matter. As to the qualification of guardians, the Act repeals all enactments on the subject, including those in local Acts, and requires that the guardians shall either be parochial electors, or have resided in the union for the twelve months preceding the election. Women, therefore, are qualified, whether married or single, and whether on the register or not. In the case of a borough there is an alternative qualification. Any person who is qualified to be a councillor for the borough will be qualified to be a guardian for any parish wholly or partly in the borough, although he may not be a parochial elector of, or resident in the parish. It is difficult to state the qualification for the office of town councillor very briefly; but generally any *man* is qualified who, for the twelve months preceding the 15th July in any year, has occupied and been rated for any house, shop, or other building in the borough, and has resided for that time in the borough or within seven miles of it. In certain cases, however, persons resident within 15 miles of the borough are qualified to be councillors, and therefore guardians of any parish in the borough (45 & 46 Vict. c. 50, ss. 9, 11).

It can scarcely be said under these circumstances that the choice of guardians for a parish in a borough is not wide, although it is to be noticed that this alternative qualification is not one which is applicable to women.

The electors of the guardians will be the parochial electors, each of whom will have one vote, and no more, for each of the number of guardians to be elected. Married women can vote, if duly qualified. There will be no proxy vote. The election is to be conducted, on the lines of a municipal election, in accordance with rules to be framed by the Local Government Board.* Every newly-elected guardian will be required to make a declaration accepting office, or pay a fine. The term of office of guardians will everywhere be three years, but the system of retirement will not be uniform, as in this particular a kind of local option is to be allowed as between the simultaneous retirement of all the guardians triennially, and the retirement of one-third every year. Appeals against elections of guardians will no longer be made to the Local Government Board, section 8 of the Poor Law Amendment Act, 1842 (5 & 6 Vict. c. 57) being repealed by the Act. If it is desired to question the election, this will have to be done by an election petition, in the same way as in the case of a municipal election (s. 48).

Section 59 of the Act applies to the meetings and proceedings of boards of guardians certain provisions of the Public Health Act, 1875. Nothing in the section, however, is to affect any powers of the Local Government Board with respect to the proceedings of guardians. The orders of that Board

* *See* page 90 *post.*

will, therefore, still govern in the matter, so far as they go. The applied provisions (which are too lengthy to refer to in detail) will only operate so far as they are not inconsistent with those orders.

The reason for dealing with the matters above referred to in the present Act becomes apparent when we consider that the administration of the poor-law union, and of the rural sanitary district forming part of the union, has hitherto been vested practically in the same body, *i.e.*, the board of guardians. Primarily, of course, the guardians are a poor-law authority; but under the Public Health Act, 1875, the same board, excepting only the guardians elected for, and *ex-officio* guardians resident in the urban parishes, constitute the sanitary authority for the rural portion of the union. At present, therefore, there is no separate election of members of a rural sanitary authority. Guardians are elected, and the guardians, with the exceptions mentioned, form the sanitary authority. The Local Government Act, 1894, reverses this arrangement so far as the rural area is concerned, but at the same time it maintains the connection between the union and the rural sanitary district, by providing that persons shall be elected to form a "rural district council" (instead of the rural sanitary authority), and that these persons shall be the representatives of the rural parishes on the board of guardians.

Guardians, as such, will only be elected for urban parishes. It is obvious that it is a necessary feature of the scheme that guardians and rural district councillors should have the same qualification, that they should be elected in the same way and by the same class of electors, and that their term of office should be the same. Apart from this, the effect of setting up within the union bodies elected on a wide popular basis like the new district councils, might, if the qualification and election of the guardians were not dealt with, be to place the latter in a position in which their influence would be impaired by reason of the less popular principle of their constitution.

It remains to be added that the election and retirement of the first guardians elected under the Act are provided for by sections 79 and 84. The election will probably take place about the end of November, 1894.* The date, however, is not yet definitively settled. The present guardians will in all cases continue in office, without re-election, until the guardians and rural district councillors elected under the new arrangement come into office. It should be noted that, even where the guardians are at present elected triennially, and the triennial period has not expired, there will be an election in November next, either of guardians or of rural district councillors, for every parish in the union. An entirely new board,

* *See* page 102 *post.*

therefore, will be returned. The first subsequent retirements will take place either in April, 1896, or in April, 1898, according as the mode of retirement is by thirds or all together every third year.

The powers of the guardians are practically unaltered, except that (*a*) the Act takes away the power of the guardians to appoint assistant overseers (s. 81); and (*b*) transfers to the parish council the powers hitherto exercised by the guardians with the approval of the Local Government Board with regard to the letting, sale, or exchange of parish property (s. 6); but (*c*), on the other hand, if the parish council or parish meeting, as the case may be, fail to appoint the overseers at the proper time, the Act confers on the guardians the power to make the appointment (s. 50). Further powers may, moreover, be conferred on the board of guardians with respect to the whole or any part of an urban district by an order of the Local Government Board, under a provision in section 33, which will be referred to hereafter.*

The provisions as to district councils now demand attention.

District Councils.

In order to understand the scheme of the Act as regards district councils, it is necessary to bear in

* *See* pp. 81, 88 *post.*

mind that at present the whole of England and Wales, exclusive of the metropolis, is divided into sanitary districts, urban and rural. Urban sanitary districts are of three kinds,—boroughs, local board districts, and Improvement Act districts. The rural sanitary districts, as previously observed, are respectively so much of a poor-law union as is not included in any urban sanitary district. The sanitary authority in the case of a borough is the corporation acting by the town council, in a local board district the local board, and in an Improvement Act district the improvement commissioners. The constitution of the rural sanitary authorities has already been adverted to.* Under the new Act, very small rural sanitary districts will, for the most part, be amalgamated with neighbouring districts; and if a rural sanitary district is in two or more counties,† the part in each county will usually be formed into a separate district (ss. 24, 36). But, except in these cases, the Act does not, as a rule, interfere with the area of sanitary districts. It does, however, make extremely important changes in the constitution of sanitary authorities other than those of boroughs, and in lieu of their existing designations, it calls all sanitary authorities " district councils." In an urban sanitary district, the district council takes

* *See* page 66 *ante.*
† Here and throughout this Introduction we use the term " county " as meaning " administrative county,"

the name of the "urban district council," and a rural sanitary district will, for the future, be governed by a "rural district council." The expression "county district" is used to include both urban and rural districts. The Act also confers new powers upon the sanitary authorities.

Urban District Councils.

As regards every urban district which is not a borough, the following matters are dealt with in the Act, viz. :—

- (*a*) the constitution of the local authority;
- (*b*) the qualification for election as a member of the authority;
- (*c*) the electorate;
- (*d*) the conduct of the election; and
- (*e*) the term of office of the members.

The existing qualification for election as a member of a local board consists in being resident within the district or within seven miles of it, and being possessed of property to the value of not less than £500 or £1,000, according to the population of the district; or being rated to the poor rate in the district at £15, or in the more populous districts at £30. The electors are the ratepayers and such of the owners as have claimed to vote, the latter having the power to vote by proxy. The poll is taken by means of voting papers delivered and collected from house to house. There is plural voting. The term of office of members is three years, one-third retiring each year. There are no *ex-officio*, and, as a rule, no nominated members.

The qualification, mode of election, and term of office of improvement commissioners depend on the provisions of the special Acts under which the several commissions are constituted. In some cases these bodies may include *ex-officio* or nominated members.

The provisions in the Local Government Act, 1894, as regards both local board and Improvement Act districts are as follows:—

There are, in future, to be neither *ex-officio* nor nominated members of the sanitary authority. The existing qualifications for members of the sanitary authority are abolished, and every person, male or female, who is a parochial elector in the district, or has, during the twelve months preceding the election, resided in the district, will be qualified to be elected a district councillor, unless otherwise disqualified.* The parochial electors are to be the electors of the district councillors. All plural and proxy voting is done away with, and each elector may give one vote, and no more, for each of any number of candidates not exceeding the number of councillors to be elected. The election is to be conducted in accordance with rules which will be framed by the Local Government Board.† The councillors are to be in office

* *See*, as to disqualifications, s. 46.   † *See* page 90 *post*.

three years, and, as a rule, one-third of the council will retire each year; but the county council may provide for the retirement of all the councillors together every third year, if the district council prefer that arrangement (s. 23).

The election and retirement of the first councillors, and the first meeting of the district council, are provided for by sections 79 and 84. It seems probable that the election will take place about the end of November, 1894;* but the precise date is not yet fixed. An entirely new body of councillors will be elected on this occasion, and the existing members of the urban sanitary authority will continue to act until the new councillors take up their duties. They will then retire together. The first subsequent retirements will take place in April 1896.

The chairman of any urban district council, other than a town council, may be elected from outside their own body. If a male, and not personally disqualified,† the chairman of every urban district council (including the town council of a non-county borough), will be *ex officio* a justice of the peace for the county. The council may also appoint a vice-chairman (ss. 22, 59).

* See page 102 *post*.
† A bankrupt or a solicitor practising in the county would be disqualified (34 & 35 Vict. c. 18; 46 & 47 Vict. c. 52).

Rural District Councils.

Instead of being only the guardians under another name, as is the case with the existing rural sanitary authority, the district council of each rural district will be a separate and distinct body. The Act incorporates it, and gives it a common seal. At present, a rural sanitary authority have to use the guardians' seal. The council will consist of a chairman and councillors. The chairman must be a person qualified to be a councillor, but he may be elected from outside, and, if a male and not personally disqualified,* will be *ex-officio* a justice of the peace for the county. The council may also appoint a vice-chairman (ss. 22, 24, 59). The councillors will be elected by the parochial electors, but, if the number of elective councillors is less than five, the Local Government Board may nominate a sufficient number of persons to make up that number. Each parish in the district will elect the same number of councillors as it now elects guardians. The provisions of the Act as to the qualification of guardians, their election in accordance with rules to be made by the Local Government Board, and their term of office and mode of retirement, apply to rural district councillors also, and any person qualified to be a guardian for the union comprising the district, will be qualified to be a district councillor for the

* *See* note (*) on previous page.

district. In one respect the result, as regards the qualification for election as rural district councillor, is very curious. As stated above, under s. 20 (2), a person qualified to be elected a town councillor for a borough is qualified to be a guardian for a parish wholly or partly in that borough. Any such person therefore is qualified to be a rural district councillor. A reference to s. 11 of the Municipal Corporations Act, 1882, will show that persons not rated for property within the rural district, or having any other direct interest in it, will thus be qualified to be elected as district councillors of that district. It will indeed be possible for a person, who is rated for property in a part of the borough outside the union altogether, and who resides more than 15 miles from any part of the union, to be qualified to be a district councillor for the rural part of the union.

As previously mentioned, the persons elected as rural district councillors will represent their several parishes on the board of guardians. Guardians, as such, will not be elected for rural parishes.

As to the election and retirement of the first councillors, and the first meeting of the rural district council, sections 79 and 84 should be referred to. The arrangements are precisely the same as in the case of guardians.*

* *See* page 67 *ante.*

Powers of District Councils.

The powers of urban and rural sanitary authorities, as at present constituted, differ considerably. Very many of the enactments in the Public Health and other Acts apply only to urban authorities. But the Local Government Board have, in many cases, power to confer on a rural authority, by order, the powers of an urban authority. The following are some of the matters in relation to which sanitary authorities have jurisdiction*:—

(*a*) powers possessed by both urban and rural authorities:—

> sewerage, drainage and water supply;
> scavenging, cleansing, and the prevention and suppression of nuisances;
> prevention and notification of infectious disease;
> provision of hospitals,† mortuaries and cemeteries;

* Some of the Acts administered by sanitary authorities are adoptive only, *i.e.*, they are in force only in districts where they are adopted. Such are the Infectious Disease (Notification) Act, 1889 (52 & 53 Vict. c. 72), the Infectious Disease (Prevention) Act, 1890 (53 & 54 Vict. c. 34), the Public Health Acts Amendment Act, 1890 (53 & 54 Vict. c. 59), Part III (Working-Class Lodging Houses) of the Housing of the Working Classes Act, 1890 (53 & 54 Vict. c. 70), and the Private Street Works Act, 1892 (55 & 56 Vict. c. 57).

† As regards the provision of hospitals, *see* the Isolation Hospitals Act, 1893 (56 & 57 Vict. c. 68).

regulation of lodging-houses;

housing of the working classes (unhealthy dwelling-houses, working class lodging-houses, *i.e.* Parts II and III of the Act of 1890);

unsound food;

adulteration of food and drugs;

provision of allotments;

sanitary regulation of factories and workshops;

prevention of the pollution of streams;

registration and regulation of canal boats:

(*b*) powers possessed by urban authorities only:—

regulation of offensive trades;

maintenance of highways;

housing of the working classes (unhealthy areas, *i.e.* Part I of the Act of 1890);

regulation of streets and buildings;

lighting;

prevention of fires;

provision of parks, markets, baths and washhouses, libraries, museums, &c.;

technical education;

regulation of tramways, omnibuses and hackney carriages.

The same powers will be possessed by urban and rural district councils respectively under the new Act.

This Act not only does not take away the power of the Local Government Board to issue orders conferring urban powers on rural authorities, but it enables them (s. 25) to issue such orders on the application of a parish or county council, whereas formerly an urban powers order could only be applied for by the rural sanitary authority, or by a number of persons representing one-tenth of the net rateable value of the district, or of any contributory place therein.*

The Local Government Board may also make *general orders* giving to every rural district council any powers of an urban sanitary authority under the Public Health or other Acts. The regulation of streets and buildings is one matter, the importance of which increases every year with the increase of population, and which might, as it seems to us, very well be dealt with by a general order in this way. Orders on this subject are continually being applied for by rural sanitary authorities, as is shown by the reports of the Local Government Board; and there are other matters, also, in regard to which it is difficult to understand why rural authorities should not have the same powers as urban authorities.

Under the Highways and Locomotives (Amend-

* 38 & 39 Vict. c. 55, s. 276.

ment) Act, 1878 (41 & 42 Vict. c. 77), about forty rural sanitary authorities have been invested with the powers of highway boards with regard to the control and maintenance of the highways within their districts. Under the new Act (s. 25) every rural district council will be the highway authority for the district for which it is elected; and for this purpose sections 144 to 148 of the Public Health Act, 1875, are made to apply. The effect of these sections is as follows:—

<small>Section 144 vests in the rural district council all the powers, duties, and liabilities of surveyors of highways, and of the inhabitants in vestry assembled under the Highway Acts.

Section 145 provides for the recovery of highway rates outstanding at the date when the district council take over the powers of the surveyors.

Section 146 enables the district council to agree as to the making of new roads, to be repaired after completion at the public expense.

Section 147. The district council may construct or adopt public bridges, &c., over or under canals, railways, or tramways.

Section 148. They may enter into agreements as to the repair, cleansing, &c., of certain streets and roads.</small>

The operation of section 25 as regards highway matters may, however, be postponed in the case of any particular county or part of a county for three years, or more, from the "appointed day."*

This clause does not apply to main roads, the management of which by the county council, subject to the provisions of the Local Government

---

* As to the "appointed day," see page 102 post.

Act, 1888, will not be interfered with by the present Act.

Other new powers which are given by the Act of this year to all district councils, urban and rural alike, are set out in sections 26 and 27. The former section makes it their duty to protect public rights of way, and prevent as far as possible the stopping or obstruction of rights of way where this would be prejudicial to the district. It is also their duty to prevent encroachments on roadside wastes. There will be an appeal to the county council if a public right of way is stopped or obstructed, or an encroachment on the roadside wastes takes place, and the district council fail to perform their duty, notwithstanding the representations of the parish council in the matter.

The effect of such an appeal will be to enable the county council to transfer to themselves the powers of the district council in the matter, and take any proceedings to enforce the rights of the public which the district council might have taken. The expenses will be recoverable from the district council under s. 63.

Section 26 also contains provisions with regard to commons. These enable any district council, with the consent of the county council, to aid persons in maintaining rights of common, where the extinction of those rights would be prejudicial to the inhabitants of the district. They are likewise empowered, with the consent of the county council, to appear on any application to the Board of Agriculture under the Commons Act, 1876, for the regulation or inclosure of a common within their district, and to make representations as to the expediency or otherwise of the application, regard being had to the health, comfort, and convenience of the inhabitants of the district. They may contribute towards the cost of the improvement of the common, and purchase common rights, and in certain cases they may be invested with powers of management of commons. This is a very useful extension of the provisions of section 8 of the Commons Act, which hitherto has only been applicable to commons in or near towns with not less than 5,000 inhabitants.*

Following the precedent set in the Bill of 1888, section 27 transfers to district councils certain administrative powers of the justices. These powers relate to—

(*a*) the licensing of agricultural gang-masters;
(*b*) the grant of pawnbrokers' certificates;
(*c*) the licensing of game-dealers;
(*d*) the grant of licences for passage brokers and emigrant runners;
(*e*) the abolition of fairs and alteration of fair days;
(*f*) the execution as local authority of the

---

* *See* also some powers of parish councils in connection with commons, referred to at page 40 *ante*.

Acts relating to petroleum and infant life protection; and

(g) the licensing of knackers' yards.

In connection with this section the following references may not be out of place:—

Licences to gang-masters are granted in petty sessions. There is an appeal to quarter sessions if a licence is refused. (*See* 30 & 31 Vict. c. 130, which makes regulations with respect to the employment of children and young persons and women in agricultural gangs.) Pawnbrokers' licences can only be granted on certificates, as to character, &c., given by stipendiary magistrates or justices in petty sessions. If a certificate is refused there is an appeal to quarter sessions (35 & 36 Vict. c. 93). Licences to game-dealers are granted annually at special sessions (1 & 2 Will. IV, c. 32, s. 18). As to the grant of licences for passage broker's and emigrant runners, *see* 18 & 19 Vict. c. 119, ss. 67, 76. On the representation of the justices of any petty sessional division within which a fair is held, or of the owner of the fair, the Home Secretary may abolish the fair, or alter the date for holding it (34 & 35 Vict. c. 12; 36 & 37 Vict. c. 37). Where the justices are the local authority for executing the Petroleum Act, 1871 (34 & 35 Vict. c. 105, s. 8), and the Infant Life Protection Act, 1872 (35 & 36 Vict. c. 38), they have power to license the storing of petroleum, and they see to the keeping of a register of persons receiving infants for hire for purposes of nursing. With respect to the licensing of knackers' yards, *see* 26 Geo. III, c. 71; 7 & 8 Vict. c. 87.

Under section 33, the Local Government Board may, as regards the whole or any specified part of any urban district, transfer to the district council, or some other representative body in the district (such as a board of guardians), all or any of the following matters, viz.: the appointment of overseers and assistant overseers; the powers, duties and liabilities of overseers; and the powers, duties and liabilities of a parish council. Among other powers which may thus be conferred on an urban district council, or on some other representative body within their district, are those of making and collecting the poor rate, of hiring land compulsorily for allotments, and of appointing trustees of charities. Where the power of appointing overseers and assistant overseers, or the powers and duties of overseers are thus transferred, the powers of the vestry under the Poor Rate Assessment and Collection Act, 1869 (32 & 33 Vict. c. 41), as regards the payment of rates by owners instead of occupiers, may be similarly dealt with (s. 34).

It appears strange that most of these powers should, as regards a rural parish, be conferred on a representative body (the parish council) as a matter of course, but that in the case of an urban parish a special order of the Local Government Board should be necessary to confer the powers. It will, however, provide for cases where more than one representative body within the same district might fairly be considered to be entitled to the powers in question, and also for exceptional cases, such as that of Liverpool, where there is a select vestry whose powers include those of overseers.

Under section 64 the county council may employ any district council as their agents in the transaction of any administrative business arising in or affecting the interests of the district. They have already power to "delegate" powers to a district council, under section 28 of the Act of 1888.

Power to appoint committees and to "concur" in appointing joint committees, is given to district councils by sections 56, 57.

Meetings and Proceedings of District Councils.

Section 59 of the Act applies to all district councils except borough councils the provisions of section 199 and the first part of Schedule I of the Public Health Act, 1875.

Every district council for a district other than a borough will therefore be required to hold an annual meeting as soon as may be convenient after the 15th of April in each year, and other meetings at least once a month; they will be empowered to make regulations as to their meetings and business, and so on.

A rural district council will be entitled to the use, at all reasonable hours, of the board-room and offices of the board of guardians.

Expenses of District Councils.

The expenses of district councils are, as a rule, to be defrayed in the same way as expenses of sanitary authorities under the Public Health Acts. In a borough, however, the expenses incurred by the council in the exercise of the additional powers conferred by this Act are to be defrayed out of the borough fund or borough rate. An important modification, too, is made as regards expenses under the Act, determined by the Local Government Board to be "special expenses" of a rural district council, the effect of which is that any such expense which, if not determined to be special, would be raised as general expenses (*i.e.* by an equal assessment as poor rate of all the occupiers in the contributory place), may, if so directed by the Local Government Board, be raised as general expenses instead of by a separate rate, to which the occupiers of land would be assessable at one-fourth only. Highway expenses in a rural district are to be a charge on the whole district, unless there are local circumstances of an exceptional character (ss. 28, 29).

Application of Act to Boroughs.

The Act only applies to boroughs to a limited extent. Thus, it does not in any way interfere with the constitution, mode of election, &c., of a town council, nor does it alter the style or title of the corporation or of the council of the borough. The following provisions, however, are applicable to boroughs as well as to other urban districts, viz.:

> Section 9, as to the acquisition of land for allotments;
> section 20, as to the qualification and election of guardians;

section 26, as to rights of way and roadside wastes, and the maintenance of rights of common;

section 27, as regards certain powers of justices transferred to district councils;

section 33, empowering the Local Government Board to confer on the council, or some other representative body within the borough, the power of appointing overseers and assistant overseers, and any powers, duties, or liabilities of overseers, or of a parish council.

In the case of a borough which is not a county borough, section 22 also applies so as to make the mayor, unless personally disqualified, a justice of the peace for the county as well as for the borough.

Application of Act to London.

We have now to indicate the extent to which the Act applies to London, by which we mean the administrative county of London (including the City) as constituted for the election of the county council.

With respect to the qualification, election, &c., of guardians, we have stated at page 62 that the metropolis is included in the provisions of the Act. But there are other matters in regard to which, as affecting London, its effect is no less important than in relation to boards of guardians. Before stating what these are we may remind the reader that within that part of the county which is outside the City of London the following bodies act as " sanitary authorities " :—

    (a) in 26 separate parishes,   the vestries constituted under the Metropolis Management Acts ;

    (b) in 13 " districts " or combinations of parishes,   the district boards constituted under those Acts ;

    (c) for the parish of Woolwich,   the Woolwich Local Board.

Except in the case of Woolwich, a vestry is elected under the Metropolis Management Acts for each of the parishes outside the City, whether included in any district under a district board or not. The electors are the ratepayers without distinction of sex, and the qualification for election consists in occupying and being rated to the poor rate in respect of premises within the parish of a minimum rateable value of, usually, £40. Women, however, are not eligible for election as vestrymen. The term of office of vestrymen is three years, one-third retiring each year. The incumbent and churchwardens are *ex-officio* members, and the former is *ex-officio* chairman of the vestry. A number of auditors are elected in each parish at the same time as the vestrymen. The auditors require the same qualification as vestrymen, but their term of office is one year. The members of each district board are elected by the vestries of the parishes in the district. They, too, must be persons qualified to be vestrymen, and their term of office is three years, one-third retiring annually. Members of the Woolwich Local Board are elected in the same way and have the same qualification as members of local boards elsewhere.—This is the existing order of things.

The new Act alters it in the following particulars:—

(*a*) the qualification and mode of election of vestrymen and auditors and members of the Woolwich Local Board;

(*b*) the qualification of the electors of all these;

(*c*) the qualification of members of district boards; and

(*d*) it amends the law respecting the office of chairman of vestries and district boards and of the Woolwich Local Board.

The effect of the provisions on these subjects may be thus stated :—The Act does away with all the existing qualifications, and for the future every person not otherwise disqualified* will be eligible

* As to disqualifications, *see* s. 46.

for election as vestryman, or auditor, or member of a district board or the Woolwich Local Board, if he is a parochial elector or has for the twelve months preceding the election resided in the parish or district, as the case may be. Women, whether married or single, can now elect and be elected.

The electors in the cases of vestrymen and auditors and members of the Woolwich Local Board will be the parochial electors, and the election in these cases will be conducted in accordance with rules to be framed by the Local Government Board.* Members of district boards will be elected as heretofore. There will be no *ex-officio* chairman of any of the vestries, although, as the vestry is concerned to some extent with affairs of the Church, the incumbent and churchwardens will continue *ex-officio* members of the vestry. Each of the vestries (except those electing district boards), each district board and the Woolwich Local Board, will annually elect a chairman for the year, who, if not a woman or personally disqualified,† will *ex-officio* be a justice of the peace for the county. The term of office is not altered in any of the above cases.

The Act further provides that any metropolitan sanitary authority, or any representative body within their district—such, for instance, as a board of guardians, or in a district under

---

* See page 90 *post*. † See note page 72 *ante*.

a district board, a vestry—may apply to the Local Government Board for an order conferring on the sanitary authority, or some representative body within their district, all or any of the following matters, viz. :—

> (a) the power of appointing overseers and assistant overseers;
> (b) any powers or duties of overseers; and
> (c) any powers or duties of a parish council.

This applies not only to the parishes and districts above mentioned but to the whole of the administrative county, including the City, for which the Commissioners of Sewers are the sanitary authority.

These provisions place London on a practical equality as regards this Act with urban districts elsewhere. They do not profess to deal with the general question of the reform of London Government, but they will, we believe, be accepted as an important step in that direction.

It only remains to be stated that the first elections under the Act of vestrymen and auditors and of members of the Woolwich Local Board, will, so far as can be seen at present, take place about the end of November, 1894.* Those now in office will then, and not till then, retire. The first retirements after next November will take place

---

* *See* page 102 *post*

at the date of the annual elections in 1896, *i.e.*, in the case of vestrymen and auditors, in the month of May, and as regards the members of the Woolwich Local Board in April 1896 (ss. 79, 84).

Conduct of Elections, &c.

We have seen that under the new Act the election of—

> parish councillors (s. 3);
> guardians (s. 20);
> urban district councillors other than councillors of a borough (s. 23);
> rural district councillors (s. 24); and
> metropolitan vestrymen and auditors and members of the Woolwich Local Board (s. 31),

is to be conducted according to rules framed under the Act by the Local Government Board. Section 48 enacts that these rules shall provide, amongst other things—

> (i.) for every candidate being nominated in writing by two parochial electors as proposer and seconder, and no more;
> (ii.) for preventing an elector at an election for a union or for a district not a borough from subscribing a nomination paper or voting in more than one parish or other area in the union or district;
> (iii.) for preventing an elector at an election for a parish

INTRODUCTION. 91

divided into parish wards from subscribing a nomination paper or voting for more than one ward;

(iv.) for fixing or enabling the county council to fix the day of the poll and the hours during which the poll is to be kept open, so, however, that the poll shall always be open between the hours of six and eight in the evening;*

(v.) for the polls at elections held at the same date and in the same area being taken together, except where this is impracticable;

(vi.) for the appointment of returning officers for the elections.

The rules have yet to be issued, but it is clear from section 48 that the election will in each case be conducted so far as possible on the lines of a municipal election. This section applies, subject to any adaptations and alterations that may be made by the rules, the Ballot Act, 1872 (35 & 36 Vict. c. 33), the Municipal Elections (Corrupt and Illegal Practices) Act, 1884 (47 & 48 Vict. c. 70), and sections 74 and 75 and Part IV† of the Municipal Corporations Act, 1882 (45 & 46 Vict. c. 50), as amended by the Act of 1884, including the penal provisions of those Acts. The modifications which the Local Government Board will make in order to adapt these enactments to the circumstances of the different elections above referred to will no doubt be considerable, but, as

* As regards London, see s. 31 (1), and note thereon.

† Sections 74 and 75 of the Act of 1882 relate to "offences in relation to nomination papers" and "offences in relation to lists and elections," and Part IV to "corrupt practices and election petitions."

indicative of the general character of the elections, we may observe that in no case will the voters have voting-papers brought to their houses as is done now in the case of an election of guardians or of members of a local board: they will proceed to an appointed polling-place, and will there be furnished with ballot-papers. These they will mark in an appointed manner, and place them in the ballot-box. Any infringement of the secrecy of the ballot, or any bribery, personation of voters, treating, undue influence, or any other thing which the Acts referred to, as adapted and applied by the rules, constitute an offence against the law, will, if committed in connection with an election under the present Act, render the offender liable to penalties.

In the case of guardians, district councillors (other than borough councillors), metropolitan vestrymen and members of the Woolwich Local Board, the rules are also to adapt the provisions of the Municipal Corporations Act, 1882, with respect to the following matters, viz., the expenses of elections of town councillors (s. 140 and Sched. V of the Act of 1882), and to the acceptance of office (s. 34), re-eligibility of holders of office (s. 37), and the filling of casual vacancies (s. 40). Section 56 of the same Act is likewise to apply. It prescribes what is to be done when the number of valid nominations is respectively greater than, the same as, and less than the number of persons to be elected. The provisions as to resignation, which are contained in s. 36 of the Act of 1882, are to be applied to urban councillors, metropolitan vestrymen, and members of the Woolwich Local Board, but not to guardians. If a guardian wishes to resign he must, as now, obtain leave from the Local Government Board.* No election to fill a casual vacancy is to be held within six months before the ordinary day of retirement from the office in which the vacancy occurs. The rules may provide for the incidence of the charge for the expenses of elections of guardians being the same as heretofore, *i.e.*, the general expenses of the election may be made a charge on the common fund, while the expenses of a contest fall on the particular parish in which the contest arises. The expenses of any election under the Act are to be limited by a scale fixed by the county council, or in their default by the Local Government Board. In the case of an election of parish councillors the expenses will be defrayed, under sections 2 and 11, as expenses of the parish meeting.

The rules are to adapt the provisions of section 48 to polls consequent upon parish meetings which are taken on any matter other than the election of parish councillors.

For the candidature of any person for the district council, or the parish council, the use of school and

* 5 & 6 Vict. c. 57, s. 11. Rural district councillors are to be in the same position as regards resignation.

other rooms can be obtained free of charge for anything beyond the actual expense (including any damage to the premises, &c.) entailed upon the managers (s. 4). Under similar conditions such rooms will also be available for use by the returning officer for hearing objections to nomination papers, for taking the poll, and for counting the votes in any of the elections above mentioned (s. 48). As mentioned elsewhere, the first elections under the Act will in all probability take place about the end of November, 1894.*

Simplification of Areas.

The question now arises, how far will the Act have the effect of simplifying the areas of local government and of reducing the number of governing bodies within any given area? On the importance of this question it is impossible to lay too much stress. The unnecessary multiplication of authorities and the chaotic intersection of boundaries which at present are found everywhere throughout the country, are matters which strike both at economy and efficiency, and it is satisfactory to observe that, although the Act may not go so far in the direction of simplification as could perhaps have been wished, yet it constitutes a great advance in that direction, and provides a basis for further consolidation in the future. The principal enactments bearing on this question

* *See* page 102 *post.*

are contained in sections 1 and 24, and Part III of the Act, which deal with new areas formed under the Act, as well as with existing areas. The intention is that, so far as possible, every parish, every group of parishes, and every sanitary district shall be wholly within the same administrative county. Every urban sanitary district was brought wholly into one administrative county by section 50 of the Act of 1888, and although there is no express provision to that effect in either Act, it would be contrary to the general scheme to so alter an urban district as to cause it to overlap a county boundary. Each parish, and each group of parishes, is also to be, as a rule, within one county district. This we say is the *intention*, but there will be exceptions. The county council, "for special reasons," may permit a rural district to remain in two or more counties, or a group of parishes to be formed of parishes not all within the same county. They may also for special reasons allow a parish or group of parishes to be in more than one county district. The symmetry of the scheme will be lost if these special reasons are found to exist in very many instances; but it is characteristic of this country that, in matters affecting local government, no general plan should be uniformly applied. We may all be conscious of a desire, as Lord Salisbury has phrased it, "to have everything at right angles and on the square," but our legislators invariably save us from ourselves in this matter by making numerous exceptions possible. The object aimed at in the present case is, however, to have every area under a parish council wholly contained within the area under one district council, and every area under a district council wholly contained within one county. A sufficiently give-and-take spirit on the part of the various local authorities and others concerned, will, it may be hoped, enable this ideal arrangement to be attained in the great majority of instances.

As regards the consolidation of powers, the most noteworthy feature of the Act is the transfer of highway jurisdiction to rural district councils. Leaving out of consideration the county councils, whose jurisdiction affects main roads only, there are at present, outside London, five different classes of highway authorities. The Act reduces the number to two, viz., urban and rural district councils. Upwards of 6,800 separate highway authorities will thus ultimately be got rid of. Other provisions of the Act, such as those respecting the Adoptive Acts, have the same general object in view, and it may be assumed that the tendency of future legislation will be rather to increase the powers of one or other of the three orders of local councils now practically called into existence than to set up a new local authority for every new purpose of local government that may arise.

Powers of County Council.

It may well be questioned where, if county councils had not previously been called into existence, the framers of this Act would have found the necessary machinery for the proper working of the measure. In the establishment of parish meetings and parish councils, the grouping of parishes, and the adjustment of interlocking areas and boundaries; in making arrangements in regard to the retirement of guardians and district councillors; in dispensing additional powers to parish meetings, district councils and metropolitan sanitary authorities, and stepping into the breach where district councils fail to perform their duties; in the acquisition of land for allotments, and in almost countless other ways, the county council is made to play the part of providence in this new scheme of local government. It would be useless to attempt to enumerate all the functions, many of them involving nice discrimination and a careful feeling of the local pulse, which are thus thrust upon the elect of the county; but the provisions which will be found in sections 36 to 40, 80 and 83, are especially important. Sections 36 to 40 relate to the vital question of readjusting areas and boundaries for the due working of the scheme, and to the making of grouping orders and the establishment of parish councils where not established by the Act. Section 36 requires them to make such orders under that section as they deem necessary for the purpose of bringing the Act into operation, and section 83 enjoins them " to exercise all such of their powers as may be requisite for bringing this Act into full operation within their county *as soon as may be*." At the end of two years, if any further orders as to areas and boundaries are necessary, the Local Government Board will complete the business, unless they think well to extend the time to enable the council to do so (s. 36). Section 80 enables the council to remove any difficulties that may arise in connection with the holding of the first parish meeting of a rural parish; the first election of parish or district councillors, guardians, metropolitan vestrymen and auditors, or members of the Woolwich Local Board; or the first meeting under the Act of a parish or district council, board of guardians or metropolitan vestry, or of the Woolwich Local Board. It is to be inferred from the reports of the Local Government Board that they, under a corresponding provision in the Act of 1888, found a large amount of work thrown upon them; and it can hardly be different with the county council in the present case. It may be safely said that by the time the scheme is fairly launched, and all obstructions to its smooth working removed, the county councils will have deserved well of the State.*

* A lengthy Circular has been issued by the Local Government Board to county councils. Copies of it can be obtained from Messrs. Eyre & Spottiswoode, East Harding Street, London, E.C.

Audit of Accounts.

The accounts of

    (a) parish councils ;

    (b) parish meetings in parishes which have not parish councils ; and

    (c) district councils other than the town councils of boroughs,

will, like the accounts of county councils, guardians and other local authorities at the present time, be audited (*see* section 58) by the district auditors appointed by the Local Government Board. The audits are to be held yearly, except in the case of rural district councils, where the audit is to be half-yearly. The Local Government Board audits are extremely efficient. The auditor has power to allow or disallow any item in the accounts which come before him. He can surcharge members of local authorities with illegal expenditure which they have authorised, and any officer with sums not accounted for, or lost to the rates through carelessness or neglect; but there is an appeal from his decision in all cases to the Queen's Bench Division of the High Court, or to the Local Government Board. The Court can only decide as to the legality of his decision ; the Local Government Board have, in addition, the power to deal with a case on its merits, and to allow expenditure incurred *bonâ fide*, although it may not be strictly legal. The cost of the audit is defrayed, in part, by means of a stamp-duty on a statutory financial statement which, at each audit, every local authority has to submit to the auditor for verification. All these provisions will apply to the parish and district councils and parish meetings above referred to.

Borough accounts (except those of Tunbridge Wells and Bournemouth, which are audited by the district auditors) will, as heretofore, be audited half-yearly under the Municipal Corporations Act, 1882 (45 & 46 Vict. c. 50), by the borough auditors, two of whom are elected by the burgesses and one appointed by the mayor.

The accounts of metropolitan vestries will be audited annually by auditors elected in the manner described at page 88. The auditors of accounts of district boards in London will continue to be elected by those boards from among the auditors for the parishes in their respective districts. In this case also the audit will be annual.

Existing Officers.

Section 75 enacts that the existing officers of local authorities, whose powers are transferred to parish or district councils, shall become the officers of the new councils. In the case of a separate highway parish electing a paid surveyor, that officer appears to be within the section. Vestry clerks and assistant overseers in office, when the

Act comes into force (except assistant overseers appointed by the guardians), will become officers of the parish council. In no case is the transfer to affect an officer's tenure of office, and while he performs the same duties, he is not to suffer in pocket.

Officers of a parish or rural sanitary district divided by the Act are to hold office for each parish or district formed by the division, their salaries being borne by the respective parishes or districts in proportion to rateable value.

Orders under section 33, transferring the powers of overseers, &c., to urban district councils, metropolitan sanitary authorities and other representative bodies, are to make proper provisions as to officers.

Any existing officer affected by the Act will, if he suffers any direct pecuniary loss by abolition of office, or by diminution or loss of emoluments, be entitled to compensation in accordance with section 120 of the Local Government Act, 1888, which, with necessary modifications, is made applicable for the purposes of the present Act, and will be found in the Appendix to this volume.

Commencement of Act; the "Appointed Day."

Following the precedent established by the Act of 1888, the new Local Government Act names an "appointed day" for the Act to come into operation. This (*see* s. 84) will not be the same for all purposes. For the purposes of elections, and of parish meetings in parishes not having a parish council, it will be "the day or respective days fixed for the first elections" under the Act, "or such prior day as may be necessary for the purpose of giving notices or doing other acts preliminary to such elections"; and for the purpose of the powers, duties and liabilities of councils, or other bodies elected under the Act, "or other matters not specifically mentioned," it will be the day on which the members of such councils, or other bodies first elected under the Act, come into office. Section 84 provides that the first elections shall be held on the 8th November, 1894, or on such later date or dates in 1894 as the Local Government Board may fix, and that the persons elected shall come into office on the second Thursday after their election, or such other day, not more than seven days earlier or later, as may be fixed by or in pursuance of the rules framed by the Local Government Board. No date other than the 8th November has yet been fixed by the Department for the elections, but it seems that the new parochial register will not come into force before the 22nd November. It is stated, however, that if the Registration Acceleration Bill (introduced on the 19th April) is agreed to, it will be possible to hold the first elections within a few days after November 22. The appointed day for the purpose of the transfer of the powers and duties of justices to town councils, under sections 27 and 32, will be the 1st of November, 1894 (s. 84). In connection with this clause, Mr. Fowler stated in the House of Commons* that—

> He proposed to continue in office all existing local authorities, whether boards of guardians, London vestries, rural sanitary authorities, or whatever the local authorities might be, until the first election under this Bill had taken place. He proposed that the people should not be put to the expense of an election in the course of the spring of this year, but the Government would ask them to have an election in the autumn of this year. * * * * The difficulty would be to complete the register * * * * so as to allow the election to take place in the month of November. * * * * The Government would ask Parliament to pass a short Act accelerating the registration, and, of course, providing any additional revising barristers who might be necessary. * * * * Any attempt to have the election upon the existing register would be most unsatisfactory, if not impossible.

Mr. Shaw Lefevre's Bill is to give effect to this arrangement.

In bringing this Introduction to a conclusion, we are conscious that many points have been omitted to which, had space allowed, it would

* "Times," 6th January, 1894.

have been proper to refer. Among these the provisions relating to the adjustment of property and liabilities, the determination of questions as to the transfer of powers, and other matters will readily occur to those familiar with statutes affecting local government. We trust, however, that no salient feature has been lost sight of. Though of less bulk, the Act is much wider in scope than that of 1888, and the difficulties attending a concise statement of its effect will be appreciated on a closer study of the measure itself. The possibilities of so great a reform in its influence upon public life are incalculable, and whatever its imperfections, no Act more far-reaching in this direction could have been placed upon the Statute Book than that which establishes "Parish Councils."

THE LOCAL GOVERNMENT ACT, 1894.

An Act to make further provision for Local Government in England and Wales.

(56 & 57 Vict. c. 73.)

[5th March, 1894.]

BE it enacted by the Queen's most Excellent Majesty, by and with the advice and consent of the Lords Spiritual and Temporal, and Commons, in this present Parliament assembled, and by the authority of the same, as follows:—

PART I.

PARISH MEETINGS AND PARISH COUNCILS.

Constitution of Parish Meetings and Parish Councils.

1.—*Constitution of parish meetings and establishment of parish councils.*—(1.) There shall be a parish meeting for every rural parish, and there shall be a parish council for every rural parish which has a population of three hundred or upwards: Provided that an order of the county council in pursuance of Part III of this Act—

> (a) shall, if the parish meeting of a rural parish having a population of one hundred or upwards so resolve, provide for establishing a parish council in the parish, and may, with the consent of the parish meeting of any rural parish having a population of less than one hundred, provide for establishing a parish council in the parish; and
>
> (b) may provide for grouping a parish with some neighbouring parish or parishes under a common parish council, but with a separate parish meeting for every parish so grouped, so, however, that no parish shall be grouped without the consent of the parish meeting for that parish.*

(2.) For the purposes of this Act every parish in a rural sanitary district shall be a rural parish.

(3.) Where a parish is at the passing of this Act situate partly within and partly without a rural sanitary district, the part of the parish which is within the district, and the part which is without, shall as from the appointed day,† but subject to any alteration of area made by or in pursuance of this or any other Act,‡ be separate parishes, in like manner as if they had been constituted

---

* The principal provisions as to grouping orders and orders establishing parish councils with less than 300 inhabitants are contained in ss. 38-40.

† As to "the appointed day," see s. 84.

‡ See particularly s. 36 of the present Act, and s 57 of the Local Government Act, 1888, a copy of which will be found in the Appendix to this volume.

separate parishes under the Divided Parishes and Poor Law Amendment Act, 1876, and the Acts amending the same.*

2.—*Parish meetings.*—(1.) The parish meeting for a rural parish shall consist of the following persons, in this Act referred to as parochial electors,† and no others, namely, the persons registered in such portion either of the local government register of electors or of the parliamentary register of electors as relates to the parish.

(2.) Each parochial elector may, at any parish meeting, or at any poll consequent thereon, give one vote and no more on any question, or, in the case of an election, for each of any number of persons not exceeding the number to be elected.

(3.) The parish meeting shall assemble at least once in every year,‡ and the proceedings of every parish meeting shall begin not earlier than six o'clock in the evening.

(4.) Subject to the provisions of this Act as to any particular person being the chairman of a

---

* (39 & 40 Vict. c. 61 ; 42 & 43 Vict. c. 54 ; 45 & 46 Vict. c. 58.) The effect of sub-section (3) is that the part of the parish within the rural sanitary district and the part without will be separate parishes for practically all civil purposes, including the appointment of overseers. As to charities and the custody of documents in parishes divided by the Act, *see* s. 36 (3), and as to overseers and " existing officers " of such parishes, ss. 79 (11), 81.

† *See* p. 20 of the Introduction. The same persons will constitute the electorate in the case of parish and district councillors, guardians of the poor, metropolitan vestrymen and auditors, and members of the Woolwich Local Board. *See* ss. 3, 20, 23, 24, 31.

‡ The date for the meeting is fixed by Sched. I, Part I.

parish meeting, the meeting may choose their own chairman.*

(5.) A poll consequent on a parish meeting shall be taken by ballot.†

(6.) The reasonable expenses of and incidental to the holding of a parish meeting or the taking of a poll consequent thereon shall be defrayed as hereinafter provided.‡

(7.) With respect to parish meetings the provisions in the First Schedule to this Act shall have effect.

3.—*Constitution of parish council.*—(1.) The parish council for a rural parish shall be elected from among the parochial electors of that parish or persons who have during the whole of the twelve months preceding the election resided in the parish, or within three miles thereof, and shall consist of a chairman and councillors, and the number of councillors shall be such as may be fixed from time to time by the county council, not being less than five nor more than fifteen.

(2.) No person shall be disqualified by sex or marriage for being elected or being a member of a parish council.§

---

* When present, the chairman of the parish council will usually be the chairman of the parish meeting (s. 45).

† The poll will be conducted in accordance with rules framed by the Local Government Board. It must always be open between 6 and 8 p.m. (ss. 3, 48).

‡ The expenses are to be paid by the parish council (if any) under s. 11, and are to include any expense or damage to which s. 4 (2) applies.

§ *See*, as to disqualifications, s. 46 of this Act. In certain cases the disqualification of a parish councillor, or of a candidate for election as such, may be removed by the county council. (*See* s. 46 (3).)

PARISH COUNCILS. 109

(3.) The term of office of a parish councillor shall be one year.

(4.) On the fifteenth day of April in each year (in this Act referred to as the ordinary day of coming into office of councillors) the parish councillors shall go out of office, and their places shall be filled by the newly-elected councillors.

(5.) The parish councillors shall be elected by the parochial electors of the parish.*

(6.) The election of parish councillors shall, subject to the provisions of this Act, be conducted according to rules framed under this Act for that purpose by the Local Government Board.

(7.) The parish councils hall in every year, on or within seven days after the ordinary day of coming into office of councillors† hold an annual meeting.

(8.) At the annual meeting, the parish council shall elect, from their own body or from other persons qualified to be councillors of the parish, a chairman, who shall, unless he resigns, or ceases to be qualified, or becomes disqualified, continue in office until his successor is elected.‡

(9.) Every parish council shall be a body corporate by the name of the parish council, with the addition of the name of the parish, or if there is any doubt as to the latter name,§ of such name as the county council after consultation with the

---

* The election will take place at a parish meeting or at a poll consequent thereon. With regard to the rules referred to in the next sub-section, *see* s. 48.

† *i.e.*, the 15th April. (*See* sub-section (4).)

‡ He may resign under s. 47. For the disqualifications under the Act, *see* s. 46. Under Rule (11) of Schedule I, Part II, the council may elect (from their own body) a vice-chairman.

§ There would be a doubt in any case where a parish was divided under s. 1.

parish meeting of the parish direct, and shall have perpetual succession, and may hold land for the purposes of their powers and duties without licence in mortmain; and any act of the council may be signified by an instrument executed at a meeting of the council, and under the hands or, if an instrument under seal is required, under the hands and seals, of the chairman presiding at the meeting and two other members of the council.

(10.) With respect to meetings of parish councils the provisions in the First Schedule to this Act shall have effect.

4.—*Use of schoolroom.*—(1.) In any rural parish* in which there is no suitable public room vested in the parish council or in the chairman of a parish meeting and the overseers which can be used free of charge for the purposes in this section mentioned, the parochial electors and the parish council shall be entitled to use, free of charge, at all reasonable times, and after reasonable notice, for the purpose of—

- (*a*) the parish meeting or any meeting of the parish council; or
- (*b*) any inquiry for parochial purposes by the Local Government Board or any other Government department or local authority; or
- (*c*) holding meetings convened by the chairman of the parish meeting or by the parish council, or if as to allotments in the manner prescribed by the Allotments Act, 1890, or otherwise as the Local

* Note that this section does not apply to parishes in urban districts.

Government Board may by rule prescribe, to discuss any question relating to allotments, under the Allotments Acts, 1887 and 1890, or under this Act; or

(d) the candidature of any person for the district council or the parish council; or

(e) any committee or officer appointed, either by the parish meeting or council or by a county or district council, to administer public funds within or for the purposes of the parish

any suitable room in the schoolhouse of any public elementary school receiving a grant out of moneys provided by Parliament, and any suitable room the expense of maintaining which is payable out of any local rate :*

Provided that this enactment shall not authorise the use of any room used as part of a private dwelling-house, nor authorise any interference with the school hours of an elementary day or evening school, nor, in the case of a room used for the administration of justice or police, with the hours during which it is used for these purposes.

(2.) If, by reason of the use of the room for any of the said purposes, any expense is incurred by the persons having control over the room, or any damage is done to the room or to the building of which the room is part or its appurtenances, or the furniture of the room or the apparatus for instruction, the expense or damage shall be defrayed as

---

* Precedents for the use of schoolrooms and other rooms which are maintained at the cost of the rates are to be found in the Ballot Act, 1872 (35 & 36 Vict. c. 33, s. 6), and the Allotments Acts, 1887 & 1890 (50 & 51 Vict. c. 48, s. 9; 53 & 54 Vict. c. 65, s. 5).

part of the expenses of the parish meeting or parish council* or inquiry as the case may be; but when the meeting is called for the purpose of the candidature of any person, such expense or damage shall be reimbursed to the parish meeting or the parish council by the persons by whom or on whose behalf the meeting is convened.

(3.) If any question arises under this section as to what is reasonable or suitable, it may be determined, in the case of a schoolhouse by the Education Department, in the case of a room used for the administration of justice or police by a Secretary of State, and in any other case by the Local Government Board.

Powers and Duties of Parish Councils and Parish Meetings.

5.—*Parish council to appoint overseers.*—(1.) The power and duty of appointing overseers of the poor, and the power of appointing and revoking the appointment of an assistant overseer, for every rural parish having a parish council, shall be transferred to and vested in the parish council, and that council shall in each year, at their annual meeting, appoint the overseers of the parish, and shall as soon as may be fill any casual vacancy occurring in the office of overseer of the parish, and shall in either case forthwith give written notice thereof in the prescribed form to the board of guardians.†

* *i.e.* as provided by s. 11.

† If the guardians do not receive notice within three weeks after the 15th April, or after the occurrence of a vacancy, they are to make the appointment or fill the vacancy themselves (s. 50).

(2.) As from the appointed day—

(*a*) the churchwardens of every rural parish shall cease to be overseers,* and an additional number of overseers may be appointed to replace the churchwardens, and

(*b*) references in any Act to the churchwardens and overseers shall, as respects any rural parish, except so far as those references relate to the affairs of the church, be construed as references to the overseers, and

(*c*) the legal interest in all property vested either in the overseers or in the churchwardens and overseers of a rural parish, other than property connected with the affairs of the church, or held for an ecclesiastical charity, shall, if there is a parish council, vest in that council, subject to all trusts and liabilities affecting the same, and all persons concerned shall make or concur in making such transfers, if any, as are requisite for giving effect to this enactment.†

6.—*Transfer of certain powers of vestry and other authorities to parish council.*—(1.) Upon the parish council of a rural parish coming into office, there shall be transferred to that council:—

(*a*) The powers, duties, and liabilities of the vestry of the parish except—

---

* Churchwardens are at present *ex-officio* overseers by virtue of 43 Eliz. c. 2.

† *See* 59 Geo. III, c. 12, s. 17, by which parish property is vested in the churchwardens and overseers for the time being. "Ecclesiastical charity" is defined by s. 75.

(i.) so far as relates to the affairs of the church or to ecclesiastical charities; and

(ii.) any power, duty, or liability transferred by this Act from the vestry to any other authority :*

(*b*) The powers, duties, and liabilities of the churchwardens of the parish, except so far as they relate to the affairs of the church or to charities, or are powers and duties of overseers, but inclusive of the obligations of the churchwardens with respect to maintaining and repairing closed churchyards wherever the expenses of such maintenance and repair are repayable out of the poor rate under the Burial Act, 1855 :† Provided that such obligations shall not in the case of any particular parish be deemed to attach, unless or until the churchwardens subsequently to the passing of this Act shall give a certificate, as in the Burial Act, 1855, provided, in order to obtain the repayment of such expenses out of the poor rate.

(*c*) The powers, duties, and liabilities of the overseers or of the churchwardens and overseers of the parish with respect to—

(i.) appeals or objections by them in respect of the valuation list, or appeals in respect of the poor rate, or county

---

* *i e.* to the parish meeting, or to the rural district council under s. 25.

† (18 & 19 Vict. c. 128.) *See* page 35 of our Introduction.

POWERS OF PARISH COUNCIL.

  rate, or the basis of the county rate ;*
and

 (ii.) the provision of parish books and of a vestry room or parochial office, parish chest, fire engine, fire escape, or matters relating thereto ;† and

 (iii.) the holding or management of parish property, not being property relating to affairs of the church or held for an ecclesiastical charity, and the holding or management of village greens, or of allotments, whether for recreation grounds or for gardens or otherwise for the benefit of the inhabitants or any of them,‡

(d) The powers exerciseable with the approval of the Local Government Board by the board of guardians for the poor law union comprising the parish in respect of the sale, exchange, or letting of any parish property.§

---

 * As to objections and appeals by overseers against valuation lists, *see* 25 & 26 Vict. c. 103, ss. 18, 32. Notices of appeals against poor rates are to be given to the churchwardens and overseers (17 Geo. II, c. 38, s. 4 ; 41 Geo. III, c 23, s. 4 ; 6 & 7 Will. IV, c. 96, s. 6). As to appeals against the county rate and the basis of that rate, *see* 15 & 16 Vict. c. 81, ss. 17–19, 22.

 † As to the several matters mentioned in this paragraph, *see* 58 Geo. II, c 69, s. 2 ; 13 & 14 Vict. c. 57, ss. 1–5 ; 24 & 25 Vict. c. 125 ; 30 & 31 Vict. c. 106, s. 29.

 ‡ *See* 8 & 9 Vict. c. 118, ss. 73–75, 92, 108–112 ; 2 & 3 Will. IV, c. 42 ; 20 & 21 Vict. c. 31, s. 12 ; 36 & 37 Vict c. 19 ; 39 and 40 Vict. c. 56, and page 37 of the Introduction.

 § *See* 5 & 6 Will. IV, c. 69, s. 3. For the consent of the owners and ratepayers now required under that Act, s. 52 substitutes the consent of the parish meeting.

(2.) A parish council shall have the same power of making any complaint or representation as to unhealthy dwellings or obstructive buildings as is conferred on inhabitant householders by the Housing of the Working Classes Act, 1890,* but without prejudice to the powers of such householders.

(3.) A parish council shall have the same power of making a representation with respect to allotments, and of applying for the election of allotment managers, as is conferred on parliamentary electors by the Allotments Act, 1887, or the Allotments Act, 1890, but without prejudice to the powers of those electors.

(4.) Where any Act constitutes any persons wardens for allotments, or authorises or requires the appointment or election of any wardens committee or managers for the purpose of allotments, then, after a parish council for the parish interested in such allotments comes into office, the powers and duties of the wardens, committee, or managers shall be exercised and performed by the parish council, and it shall not be necessary to make the said appointment or to hold the said election, and for the purpose of section sixteen of the Small Holdings Act, 1892, two members of the parish council shall be substituted for allotment managers or persons appointed as allotment managers.†

* (53 & 54 Vict. c. 70.) See p. 38 of the Introduction.

† S. 16 of the Small Holdings Act (55 & 56 Vict. c. 31) provides for the delegation by the county council of the management of small holdings to a committee consisting partly of allotment managers under the Allotments Act, 1887, or persons appointed in like manner as allotment managers. The incumbent, one churchwarden and two ratepayers are constituted

7.—*Transfer of powers under Adoptive Acts.*—
(1.) As from the appointed day, in every rural parish the parish meeting shall, exclusively, have the power of adopting any of the following Acts, inclusive of any Acts amending the same (all which Acts are in this Act referred to as " the Adoptive Acts "); namely,—

(*a*) The Lighting and Watching Act, 1833;
(*b*) The Baths and Washhouses Acts, 1846 to 1882;
(*c*) The Burial Acts, 1852 to 1885;
(*d*) The Public Improvements Act, 1860;
(*e*) The Public Libraries Act, 1892.*

(2.) Where under any of the said Acts a particular majority is required for the adoption or abandonment of the Act, or for any matter under such Act, the like majority of the parish meeting or, if a poll is taken, of the parochial electors, shall be required, and where under any of the said Acts the opinion of the voters is to be ascertained by voting papers, the opinion of the parochial electors shall be ascertained by a poll taken in manner provided by this Act.

(3.) Where under any of the said Acts the consent or approval of, or other act on the part of,

---

wardens for the management of allotments for the labouring poor (8 & 9 Vict. c. 118, s. 108). The vestry appoint annually a committee for the purposes of fuel allotments under 2 & 3 Will. IV, c. 42 (36 & 37 Vict. c. 19). Allotment managers are either appointed by the sanitary authority under s. 6 or elected by the parliamentary electors under s. 9 of the Act of 1887.

* (3 & 4 Will. 4, c. 90.—9 & 10 Vict. c. 74; 45 & 46 Vict. c. 30. —15 & 16 Vict. c. 85; 48 & 49 Vict. c. 21.—23 & 24 Vict. c. 30. —55 & 56 Vict. c. 53.) We have dealt somewhat in detail with these Acts in our Introduction, pp. 42 to 45.

the vestry of a rural parish is required in relation to any expense or rate, the parish meeting shall be substituted for the vestry, and for this purpose the expression "vestry" shall include any meeting of ratepayers or voters.

(4.) Where there is power to adopt any of the Adoptive Acts, for a part only of a rural parish, the Act may be adopted by a parish meeting held for that part.*

(5.) Where the area under any existing authority acting within a rural parish in the execution of any of the Adoptive Acts is co-extensive with the parish, all powers, duties, and liabilites of that authority shall, on the parish council coming into office, be transferred to that council.†

(6.) This Act shall not alter the incidence of charge of any rate levied to defray expenses incurred under any of the Adoptive Acts, and any such rate shall be made and charged as heretofore, and any property applicable to the payment of such expenses shall continue to be so applicable.

(7.) When any of the Adoptive Acts is adopted for the whole or part of a rural parish after the appointed day, and the parish has a parish council, the parish council shall be the authority for the execution of the Act.

(8.) For the purposes of this Act the passing of a resolution to provide a burial ground under the Burial Acts, 1852 to 1885, shall be deemed an adoption of those Acts.

* As to parish meetings for parts of parishes *see* s. 49.

† Areas under any authority which are not co-extensive with the parish are provided for by s. 53. The same section provides for the alteration of the boundaries of areas under these authorities.

8.—*Additional powers of parish council.*—(1.) A parish council shall have the following additional powers, namely, power—

- (*a*) to provide or acquire buildings for public offices and for meetings and for any purposes connected with parish business or with the powers or duties of the parish council or parish meeting; and
- (*b*) to provide or acquire land for such buildings and for a recreation ground and for public walks;* and
- (*c*) to apply to the Board of Agriculture under section nine of the Commons Act, 1876;† and
- (*d*) to exercise with respect to any recreation ground, village green, open space, or public walk, which is for the time being under their control, or to the expense of which they have contributed, such powers as may be exercised by an urban authority under section one hundred and sixty-four of the Public Health Act, 1875, or section forty-four of the Public Health Acts Amendment Act, 1890, in relation to recreation grounds or public walks, and sections one hundred and eighty-three to one hundred and eighty-six of the Public Health Act, 1875,‡ shall apply accordingly as if the parish council were a local

---

* As to the acquisition of land for the purposes of the parish council, *see* s. 9.

† 39 & 40 Vict. c. 56.

‡ Ss. 183 to 186 of the Public Health Act, 1875, relate to the making and confirmation of byelaws. The Local Government Board have issued model byelaws under s. 164 of that Act.

authority within the meaning of those sections, and

(e) to utilise any well, spring, or stream within their parish and provide facilities for obtaining water therefrom, but so as not to interfere with the rights of any corporation or person ;* and

(f) to deal with any pond, pool, open ditch, drain, or place containing, or used for the collection of, any drainage, filth, stagnant water, or matter likely to be prejudicial to health, by draining, cleansing, covering it, or otherwise preventing it from being prejudicial to health, but so as not to interfere with any private right or the sewage or drainage works of any local authority ;* and

(g) to acquire by agreement any right of way, whether within their parish or an adjoining parish, the acquisition of which is beneficial to the inhabitants of the parish or any part thereof† ; and

(h) to accept and hold any gifts of property, real or personal, for the benefit of the inhabitants of the parish or any part thereof; and

(i) to execute any works (including works of maintenance or improvement) incidental to or consequential on the exercise of any of the foregoing powers, or in relation to

---

* These two paragraphs should be read with subsection (3) and s. 16. The council cannot acquire land for water supply compulsorily (s. 9 (15)).

† Other provisions as to rights of way are contained in ss 13, 19, 26. The council cannot use compulsory powers for acquiring rights of way (s. 9 (15)).

any parish property, not being property relating to affairs of the church or held for an ecclesiastical charity; and

(*k*) to contribute towards the expense of doing any of the things above mentioned, or to agree or combine with any other parish council to do or contribute towards the expense of doing any of the things above mentioned.

(2.) A parish council may let, or, with the consent of the parish meeting, sell or exchange, any land or buildings vested in the council, but the power of letting for more than a year and the power of sale or exchange shall not be exercised, in the case of property which has been acquired at the expense of any rate, or is at the passing of this Act applied in aid of any rate, or would but for want of income be so applied, without the consent of the Local Government Board, or in any other case without such consent or approval as is required under the Charitable Trusts Acts, 1853 to 1891,* for the sale of charity estates, provided that the consent or approval required under those Acts shall not be required for the letting for allotments of land vested in the parish council.

(3.) Nothing in this section shall derogate from any obligation of a district council with respect to the supply of water or the execution of sanitary works.

(4.) Notice of any application to the Board of Agriculture in relation to a common shall be served upon the council of every parish in which any part of the common to which the application relates is situate.†

---

* 16 & 17 Vict. c. 137; 54 & 55 Vict. c. 17.

† *See* the Commons Act, 1876 (39 & 40 Vict. c. 56).

9.—*Powers for acquisition of land.*—(1.) For the purpose of the acquisition of land by a parish council the Lands Clauses Acts shall be incorporated with this Act, except the provisions of those Acts with respect to the purchase and taking of land otherwise than by agreement, and section one hundred and seventy-eight of the Public Health Act, 1875, shall apply as if the parish council were referred to therein.*

(2.) If a parish council are unable to acquire by agreement and on reasonable terms suitable land for any purpose for which they are authorised to acquire it, they may represent the case to the county council, and the county council shall inquire into the representation.

(3.) If on any such representation, or on any proceeding under the Allotments Acts, 1887 and 1890,† a county council are satisfied that suitable land for the said purpose of the parish council or for the purpose of allotments (as the case may be), cannot be acquired on reasonable terms by voluntary agreement, and that the circumstances are such as to justify the county council in proceeding under this section, they shall cause such public inquiry to be made in the parish, and such notice to be given both in the parish and to the owners, lessees, and occupiers of the land proposed to be taken as may be prescribed,‡ and all persons interested shall be permitted to attend at the

---

* This merely enables the Duchy of Lancaster to sell land to the parish council.

† 50 & 51 Vict. c. 48; 53 & 54 Vict. c. 65.

‡ "Prescribed" means prescribed by order of the Local Government Board (s. 75). Section 9 (7) contemplates the issue by the Board of "regulations" for the purposes of this section.

inquiry, and to support or oppose the taking of the land.

(4.) After the completion of the inquiry, and considering all objections made by any persons interested, the county council may make an order, for putting in force, as respects the said land or any part thereof, the provisions of the Lands Clauses Acts with respect to the purchase and taking of land otherwise than by agreement.

(5.) If the county council refuse to make any such order, the parish council, or, if the proceeding is taken on the petition of the district council, then the district council, may petition the Local Government Board, and that Board after local inquiry may, if they think proper, make the order, and this section shall apply as if the order had been made by the county council. Any order made under this subsection overruling the decision of the county council shall be laid before Parliament by the Local Government Board.

(6.) A copy of any order made under this section shall be served in the prescribed manner, together with a statement that the order will become final and have the effect of an Act of Parliament, unless within the prescribed period a memorial by some person interested is presented to the Local Government Board praying that the order shall not become law without further inquiry.

(7.) The order shall be deposited with the Local Government Board, who shall inquire whether the provisions of this section and the prescribed regulations have been in all respects complied with; and if the Board are satisfied that this has been done, then, after the prescribed period—

(*a*) If no memorial has been presented, or if

every such memorial has been withdrawn, the Board shall, without further inquiry, confirm the order :*

(b) If a memorial has been presented, the Local Government Board shall proceed to hold a local inquiry, and shall, after such inquiry, either confirm, with or without amendment, or disallow the order :

(c) Upon any such confirmation the order, and if amended as so amended, shall become final and have the effect of an Act of Parliament, and the confirmation by the Local Government Board shall be conclusive evidence that the requirements of this Act have been complied with, and that the order has been duly made, and is within the powers of this Act.

(8.) Sections two hundred and ninety-three to two hundred and ninety-six, and subsections (1) and (2) of section two hundred and ninety-seven of the Public Health Act, 1875,† shall apply to a

---

* In a case where no memorial is presented, or the memorial is withdrawn, the Board, assuming that the order has been duly made in accordance with the Act and regulations, will have no alternative but to confirm the order; they cannot amend it. But, under paragraph (b), if a memorial is presented the Board, in confirming the order, may amend it, or they may disallow it.

† Section 293 gives the Board power to direct inquiries.

Section 294 enables them to make orders as to the costs of inquiries, and the parties by whom the costs are to be borne.

Section 295. Orders of Board conclusive, and to be published.

Section 296. Powers of Board's inspectors as to examination, &c. of witnesses, production of documents, &c.

Section 297. (1.) Order not to be made by Board without previous advertisement in local newspaper.

(2.) Before making order, inquiry to be held and objections considered.

local inquiry held by the Local Government Board for the purposes of this section, as if those sections and subsections were herein re-enacted, and in terms made applicable to such inquiry.

(9.) The order shall be carried into effect, when made on the petition of a district council, by that council, and in any other case by the county council.

(10.) Any order made under this section for the purpose of the purchase of land otherwise than by agreement shall incorporate the Lands Clauses Acts and sections seventy-seven to eighty-five of the Railways Clauses Consolidation Act, 1845,* with the necessary adaptations, but any question of disputed compensation shall be dealt with in the manner provided by section three of the Allotments Act, 1887, and provisoes (a), (b), and (c) of subsection (4) of that section are incorporated with this section and shall apply accordingly :† Provided that in determining the amount of disputed compensation, the arbitrator shall not make any additional allowance in respect of the purchase being compulsory.

(11.) At any inquiry or arbitration held under this section the person or persons holding the inquiry or arbitration shall hear any authorities or parties interested by themselves or their agents,

* (8 & 9 Vict. c. 20.) These sections prevent the working of mines under or near a railway, in such a way as to cause damage to the latter, while at the same time they provide for compensation to the owner for any loss which he may sustain through their provisions.

† Any question of disputed compensation is under s. 3 of the Act of 1887 to be referred to a single arbitrator appointed by the parties, or, if they do not agree, by the Local Government Board.

and shall hear witnesses, but shall not, except in such cases as may be prescribed, hear counsel or expert witnesses.

(12.) The person or persons holding a public inquiry for the purposes of this section on behalf of a county council shall have the same powers as an inspector or inspectors of the Local Government Board when holding a local inquiry; and section two hundred and ninety-four of the Public Health Act, 1875,* shall apply to the costs of inquiries held by the county council for the purpose of this section as if the county council were substituted for the Local Government Board.

(13.) Subsection (2) of section two, if the land is taken for allotments, and, whether it is or is not so taken, subsections (5), (6), (7), and (8) of section three of the Allotments Act, 1887, and section eleven of that Act, and section three of the Allotments Act, 1890, are incorporated with this section, and shall, with the prescribed adaptations, apply accordingly.†

* *See* note to subsection (8).
† These enactments are to the following effect:—
Allotments Act, 1887.
Section 2 (2). Land not to be acquired except at such price that the expenses may reasonably be expected to be recouped out of the rents obtained for the allotments.
Section 3 (5). [Construction of enactments.]
(6). An order for compulsory purchase not to be made as respects land required for the amenity or convenience of a dwelling-house, or land belonging to and required by a railway or canal company. As far as practicable, the taking an undue or inconvenient quantity of land from any one owner is to be avoided.
(7). Persons are authorised to lease land for not more than thirty-five years.

(14.) Where the land is acquired otherwise than for allotments, it shall be assured to the parish council; and any land purchased by a county council for allotments under the Allotments Acts, 1887 and 1890, and this Act, or any of them, shall be assured to the parish council, and in that case sections five to eight of the Allotments Act, 1887,* shall apply as if the parish council were the sanitary authority.

(15.) Nothing in this section shall authorise the parish council to acquire otherwise than by agreement any land for the purpose of any supply of water, or of any right of way.†

(16.) In this section the expression "allotments" includes common pasture where authorised to be acquired under the Allotments Act, 1887.‡

(17.) Where, under the Allotments Act, 1890, the Allotments Act, 1887, applies to the purchase of land by the county council, that Act shall apply as amended by this section, and the parish council shall have the like power of petitioning the county council as is given to six parliamentary electors by section two of the Allotments Act, 1890.§

(8). No order to be made for purchasing any right to coal or metalliferous ore.

Section 11. [Sale of superfluous or unsuitable land.]

Allotments Act, 1890.

Section 3. County council to appoint a standing committee for the purposes of allotments.

* These sections relate to the improvement and adaptation of the land for allotments, the management, letting and use of allotments, and the recovery of rent and possession from allottees.

† See s. 8, subsection (1). ‡ See s. 12 of the Act of 1887.

§ i.e. they may petition if after a representation by the parish council or by six parliamentary electors or ratepayers, the district

(18.) This section shall apply to a county borough with the necessary modifications, and in particular with the modification that the order shall be both made and confirmed by the Local Government Board and shall be carried into effect by the council of the county borough.

(19.) The expenses of a county council incurred under this section shall be defrayed in like manner as in the case of a local inquiry by a county council under this Act.*

10.—*Hiring of land for allotments.*—(1.) The parish council shall have power to hire land for allotments, and if they are satisfied that allotments are required, and are unable to hire by agreement on reasonable terms suitable land for allotments, they shall represent the case to the county council, and the county council may make an order authorising the parish council to hire compulsorily for allotments, for a period not less than fourteen years nor more than thirty-five years, such land in or near the parish as is specified in the order, and the order shall, as respects confirmation and otherwise, be subject to the like provisions as if it were an order of the county council made under the last preceding section of this Act, and that section shall apply as if it were herein re-enacted with the substitution of " hiring " for " purchase " and with the other necessary modifications.

(2.) A single arbitrator, who shall be appointed in accordance with the provisions of section three

council fail to acquire sufficient land of a suitable character for allotments.

* *i.e.* as provided by section 72.

of the Allotments Act, 1887,* and to whom the provisions of that section shall apply, shall have power to determine any question—

(a) as to the terms and conditions of the hiring; or
(b) as to the amount of compensation for severance; or
(c) as to the compensation to any tenant upon the determination of his tenancy; or
(d) as to the apportionment of the rent between the land taken by the parish council and the land not taken from the tenant; or
(e) as to any other matter incidental to the hiring of the land by the council, or the surrender thereof at the end of their tenancy;

but the arbitrator in fixing the rent shall not make any addition in respect of compulsory hiring.

(3.) The arbitrator, in fixing rent or other compensation, shall take into consideration all the circumstances connected with the land, and the use to which it might otherwise be put by the owner during the term of hiring, and any depreciation of the value to the tenant of the residue of his holding caused by the withdrawal from the holding of the land hired by the parish council.

(4.) Any compensation awarded to a tenant in respect of any depreciation of the value to him of the residue of his holding caused by the withdrawal from the holding of the land hired by the parish council shall as far as possible be provided

---

* *i.e.* by the parties, or, if the parties do not agree, by the Local Government Board.

for by taking such compensation into account in fixing, as the case may require, the rent to be paid by the parish council for the land hired by them, and the apportioned rent, if any, to be paid by the tenant for that portion of the holding which is not hired by the parish council.

(5.) The award of the arbitrator or a copy thereof, together with a report signed by him as to the condition of the land taken by the parish council, shall be deposited and preserved with the public books, writings, and papers of the parish,* and the owner for the time being of the land shall at all reasonable times be at liberty to inspect the same and to take copies thereof.

(6.) Save as hereinafter mentioned, sections five to eight of the Allotments Act, 1887,† shall apply to any allotment hired by a parish council in like manner as if that council were the sanitary authority and also the allotment managers:

Provided that the parish council—

(a) may let to one person an allotment or allotments exceeding one acre,‡ but, if the land is hired compulsorily, not exceeding in the whole four acres of pasture or one acre of arable and three acres of pasture; and

(b) may permit to be erected on the allotment any stable, cowhouse, or barn;§ and

(c) shall not break up, or permit to be broken up, any permanent pasture, without the assent in writing of the landlord.

* The deposit of the public books, writings, &c., of the parish is provided for in s. 17.

† *See* note to section 9 (14).

‡ One acre was the limit under the Act of 1887.

§ Such buildings were not permitted by the Act of 1887.

(7.) On the determination of any tenancy created by compulsory hiring a single arbitrator who shall be appointed in accordance with the provisions of section three of the Allotments Act, 1887,* shall have power to determine as to the amount due by the landlord for compensation for improvements, or by the parish council for depreciation, but such compensation shall be assessed in accordance with the provisions of the Agricultural Holdings (England) Act, 1883.†

(8.) The order for compulsory hiring may apply, with the prescribed adaptations, such of the provisions of the Lands Clauses Acts (including those relating to the acquisition of land otherwise than by agreement) as appear to the county council or Local Government Board sufficient for carrying into effect the order, and for the protection of the persons interested in the land and of the parish council.

(9.) Nothing in this section shall authorise the compulsory hiring of any mines or minerals, or confer any right to take, sell, or carry away any gravel, sand, or clay, or authorise the hiring of any land which is already owned or occupied as a small holding within the meaning of the Small Holdings Act, 1892.‡

(10.) If the land hired under this section shall at any time during the tenancy thereof by the parish council be shown to the satisfaction of the county council to be required by the landlord for the purpose of working and getting the mines, minerals, or surface minerals thereunder, or for any road or work to be used in connexion with such

---

* *See* note to subsection (2).   † 46 & 47 Vict. c. 61.
‡ 55 & 56 Vict. c. 31.

working or getting, it shall be lawful for the landlord of such land to resume possession thereof upon giving to the parish council twelve calendar months' previous notice in writing of his intention so to do, and upon such resumption the landlord shall pay to the parish council and to the allotment holders of the land for the time being such sum by way of compensation for the loss of such land for the purposes of allotments as may be agreed upon by the landlord and the parish council, or in default of such agreement as may be awarded by a single arbitrator to be appointed in accordance with the provisions of section three of the Allotments Act, 1887,* and the provisions of that section shall apply to such arbitrator.

The word "landlord" in this subsection means the person for the time being entitled to receive the rent of the land hired by the parish council.

(11.) The Local Government Board shall annually lay before Parliament the report of any proceedings under this and the preceding section.

11.—*Restrictions on expenditure.*—(1.) A parish council shall not, without the consent of a parish meeting, incur expenses or liabilities which will involve a rate exceeding threepence in the pound for any local financial year,† or which will involve a loan.

(2.) A parish council shall not, without the approval of the county council, incur any expense or liability which will involve a loan.

(3.) The sum raised in any local financial year

---

* *See* note to subsection (2).

† *i.e.* the twelve months ending the 31st March. (Local Government Act, 1888, s. 73, and s. 75 of the present Act.)

by a parish council for their expenses (other than expenses under the Adoptive Acts) shall not exceed a sum equal to a rate of sixpence in the pound on the rateable value of the parish at the commencement of the year, and for the purpose of this enactment the expression " expenses " includes any annual charge, whether of principal or interest, in respect of any loan.

(4.) Subject to the provisions of this Act, the expenses of a parish council and of a parish meeting, including the expenses of any poll, shall be paid out of the poor rate; and where there is a parish council that council shall pay the said expenses of the parish meeting of the parish; and the parish council, and where there is no parish council the chairman of the parish meeting, shall, for the purpose of obtaining payment of such expenses, have the same powers as a board of guardians have for the purpose of obtaining contributions to their common fund.*

(5.) The demand note for any rate levied for defraying the expenses of a parish council or a parish meeting, together with other expenses, shall state in the prescribed form the proportion of the rate levied for the expenses of the council or meeting, and the proportion (if any) levied for the purpose of any of the Adoptive Acts.

12.—*Borrowing by parish council.*—(1.) A parish council for any of the following purposes, that is to say—

    (*a*) for purchasing any land, or building any

---

* *See* s. 4 (2) as to the expenses connected with the use of school and other rooms for meetings.

buildings, which the council are authorised to purchase or build; and

(b) for any purpose for which the council are authorised to borrow under any of the Adoptive Acts;* and

(c) for any permanent work or other thing which the council are authorised to execute or do, and the cost of which ought, in the opinion of the county council and the Local Government Board, to be spread over a term of years;

may, with the consent of the county council and the Local Government Board, borrow money in like manner and subject to the like conditions as a local authority may borrow for defraying expenses incurred in the execution of the Public Health Acts, and sections two hundred and thirty-three, two hundred and thirty-four, and two hundred and thirty-six to two hundred and thirty-nine of the Public Health Act, 1875, shall apply accordingly,† except that the money shall be borrowed on the security of the poor rate and of the whole or part of the revenues of the parish council, and except that as respects the limit of the sum to be borrowed, one half of the assessable value shall be substituted for the assessable value for two years.

* Borrowing powers for the purposes of the Adoptive Acts are conferred as follows :—

    Baths and Washhouses Acts,—9 & 10 Vict. c. 74, s. 21; 41 & 42 Vict. c. 14, s. 9;

    Burial Acts,—15 & 16 Vict. c. 85, s. 20; 17 & 18 Vict. c. 87, ss. 4, 5; 18 & 19 Vict. c. 128, s. 6; 20 & 21 Vict. c. 81, s. 21;

    Public Libraries Act,—55 & 56 Vict. c. 53, s. 19.

† The effect of these enactments is stated at page 54 of the Introduction.

(2.) A county council may lend to a parish council any money which the parish council are authorised to borrow, and may, if necessary, without the sanction of the Local Government Board, and irrespectively of any limit of borrowing, raise the money by loan, subject to the like conditions and in the like manner as any other loan for the execution of their duties, and subject to any further conditions which the Local Government Board may by general or special order impose.*

(3.) A parish council shall not borrow for the purposes of any of the Adoptive Acts otherwise than in accordance with this Act, but the charge for the purpose of any of the Adoptive Acts shall ultimately be on the rate applicable to the purposes of that Act.

13.—*Footpaths and roads.*—(1.) The consent of the parish council and of the district council shall be required for the stopping, in whole or in part, or diversion, of a public right of way within a rural parish, and the consent of the parish council shall be required for a declaration that a highway in a rural parish is unnecessary for public use and not repairable at the public expense, and the parish council shall give public notice† of a resolution to give any such consent, and the resolution shall not operate—

> (a) unless it is confirmed by the parish council at a meeting held not less than two months after the public notice is given; nor

---

* As to borrowing by county councils, s. 69 of the Local Government Act, 1888, may be referred to.

† Public notices by a parish council for the purposes of this Act are to be given as provided by s. 51.

(*b*) if a parish meeting held before the confirmation resolve that the consent ought not to be given.

(2.) A parish council may, subject to the provisions of this Act with respect to restrictions on expenditure,* undertake the repair and maintenance of all or any of the public footpaths within their parish, not being footpaths at the side of a public road, but this power shall not nor shall the exercise thereof relieve any other authority or person from any liability with respect to such repair or maintenance.

14.—*Public property and charities.*†—(1.) Where trustees‡ hold any property for the purposes of a public recreation ground or of public meetings, or of allotments, whether under Inclosure Acts or otherwise, for the benefit of the inhabitants of a rural parish, or any of them, or for any public purpose connected with a rural parish, except for an ecclesiastical charity,‡ they may, with the approval of the Charity Commissioners, transfer the property to the parish council of the parish, or to persons appointed by that council, and the parish council, if they accept the transfer, or their appointees, shall hold the property on the trusts and subject to the conditions on which the trustees held the same.

(2.) Where overseers of a rural parish as such are, either alone or jointly with any other persons, trustees of any parochial charity,‡ such number of the councillors of the parish or other persons, not

---

* The reference is to s. 11.

† The remarks at page 48 of the Introduction should be read in connection with this section.

‡ *See* the definitions in s. 75.

exceeding the number of the overseer trustees, as the council may appoint, shall be trustees in their place, and, when the charity is not an ecclesiastical charity, this enactment shall apply as if the churchwardens as such were specified therein as well as the overseers.

(3.) Where the governing body of a parochial charity other than an ecclesiastical charity does not include any persons elected by the ratepayers or parochial electors or inhabitants of the parish, or appointed by the parish council or parish meeting, the parish council may appoint additional members of that governing body not exceeding the number allowed by the Charity Commissioners in each case; and if the management of any such charity is vested in a sole trustee, the number of trustees may, with the approval of the Charity Commissioners, be increased to three, one of whom may be nominated by such sole trustee and one by the parish council or parish meeting. Nothing in this subsection shall prejudicially affect the power or authority of the Charity Commissioners, under any of the Acts relating to charities, to settle or alter schemes for the better administration of any charity.

(4.) Where the vestry of a rural parish are entitled, under the trusts of a charity other than an ecclesiastical charity, to appoint any trustees or beneficiaries of the charity, the appointment shall be made by the parish council of the parish, or in the case of beneficiaries, by persons appointed by the parish council.

(5.) The draft of every scheme relating to a charity, not being an ecclesiastical charity, which affects a rural parish, shall, on or before the publication of the notice of the proposal to make an order for such scheme in accordance with section six of the Charitable Trusts Act, 1860,* be communicated to the council of the parish, and where there is no parish council to the chairman of the parish meeting, and, in the case of a council, the council may, subject to the provisions of this Act with respect to restrictions on expenditure,† and to the consent of the parish meeting, either support or oppose the scheme, and shall for that purpose have the same right as any inhabitants of a place directly affected by the scheme.

(6.) The accounts of all parochial charities, not being ecclesiastical charities, shall annually be laid before the parish meeting of any parish affected thereby, and the Charitable Trusts Amendment Act, 1855,‡ shall apply with the substitution in section forty-four of the parish meeting for the vestry, and of the chairman of the parish meeting for the churchwardens, and the names of the beneficiaries of dole charities shall be published annually in such form as the parish council, or where there is no parish council the parish meeting, think fit.

(7.) The term of office of a trustee appointed under this section shall be four years, but of the trustees first appointed as aforesaid one half, as nearly as may be, to be determined by lot, shall go out of office at the end of two years from the date of their appointment, but shall be eligible for re-appointment.

(8.) The provisions of this section with respect

---

* 23 & 24 Vict. c. 136.
† Section 11 contains the provisions referred to.
‡ 18 & 19 Vict, c, 124,

to the appointment of trustees, except so far as the appointment is transferred from the vestry, shall not apply to any charity until the expiration of forty years from the date of the foundation thereof, or, in the case of a charity founded before the passing of this Act by a donor or by several donors any one of whom is living at the passing of this Act, until the expiration of forty years from the passing of this Act, unless with the consent of the surviving donor or donors.

(9.) Whilst a person is trustee of a parochial charity he shall not, nor shall his wife or any of his children, receive any benefit from the charity.

15.—*Delegated powers of parish councils.*—A rural district council may delegate to a parish council any power which may be delegated to a parochial committee under the Public Health Acts, and thereupon those Acts shall apply as if the parish council were a parochial committee, and where such district council appoint a parochial committee consisting partly of members of the district council and partly of other persons, those other persons shall, where there is a parish council, be or be selected from the members of the parish council.

16.—*Complaint by parish council of default of district council.*—(1.) Where a parish council resolve that a rural district council ought to have provided the parish with sufficient sewers, or to have maintained existing sewers, or to have provided the parish with a supply of water in cases where danger arises to the health of the inhabitants from the insufficiency or unwholesomeness of the existing supply of water, and a proper supply can be got at a reasonable cost, or to have enforced with regard to the parish any provisions of the Public Health Acts which it is their duty to enforce, and have failed so to do, or that they have failed to maintain and repair any highway in a good and substantial manner, the parish council may complain to the county council, and the county council, if satisfied after due inquiry that the district council have so failed as respects the subject matter of the complaint, may resolve that the duties and powers of the district council for the purpose of the matter complained of shall be transferred to the county council, and they shall be transferred accordingly.*

(2.) Upon any complaint under this section the county council may, instead of resolving that the duties and powers of the rural district council be transferred to them, make such an order as is mentioned in section two hundred and ninety-nine of the Public Health Act, 1875, and may appoint a person to perform the duty mentioned in the order, and upon such appointment sections two hundred and ninety-nine to three hundred and two of the Public Health Act, 1875, shall apply with the substitution of the county council for the Local Government Board.

(3.) Where a rural district council have determined to adopt plans for the sewerage or water supply of any contributory place within the district, they shall give notice thereof to the parish council of any parish for which the works are to be provided before any contract is entered into by them for the execution of the works.

17.—*Parish officers and parish documents.*—(1.) A parish council may appoint one of their number

* In connection with subsection (1) section 63 should be read.

PARISH OFFICERS. 141

to act as clerk of the council without remuneration.

(2.) If no member of the parish council is appointed so to act, and there is an assistant overseer, he, or such one of the assistant overseers, if more than one, as may be appointed by the council, shall be the clerk of the parish council, and the performance of his duties as such shall be taken into account in determining his salary.*

(3.) If there is no assistant overseer, the parish council may appoint a collector of poor rates, or some other fit person, to be their clerk, with such remuneration as they may think fit.

(4.) A parish council shall not appoint to the office of vestry clerk.†

(5.) When a parish council act as a parochial committee by delegation from the district council‡ they shall have the services of the clerk of the district council, unless the district council otherwise direct.

(6.) The parish council may appoint one of their own number or some other person to act as treasurer without remuneration, and the treasurer shall give such security as may be required by regulations of the county council.

(7.) All documents required by statute or by standing orders of Parliament to be deposited with the parish clerk of a rural parish shall, after the election of a parish council, be deposited with the clerk, or, if there is none, with the chairman, of the parish council, and the enactments with respect to the inspection of, and taking copies of, and extracts

---

* But *see* s. 81 (2).
† An existing vestry clerk is provided for by s. 81 (2).
‡ *i.e.* under s. 15.

from, any such documents shall apply as if the clerk, or chairman, as the case may be, were mentioned therein.*

(8.) The custody of the registers of baptisms, marriages, and burials, and of all other books and documents containing entries wholly or partly relating to the affairs of the church or to ecclesiastical charities, except documents directed by law to be kept with the public books, writings, and papers of the parish, shall remain as provided by the existing law unaffected by this Act.† All other public books, writings, and papers of the parish, and all documents directed by law to be kept therewith, shall either remain in their existing custody, or be deposited in such custody as the parish council may direct. The incumbent and churchwardens on the one part, and the parish council on the other, shall have reasonable access to all such books, documents, writings, and papers, as are referred to in this subsection, and any difference as to custody or access shall be determined by the county council.

(9.) Every county council shall from time to time inquire into the manner in which the public books, writings, papers, and documents under the control of the parish council or parish meeting are kept with a view to the proper preservation thereof, and shall make such orders as they think necessary

---

* The enactments referred to impose penalties for not permitting inspection, &c.

† Registers of baptisms and burials are, under 52 Geo III, c. 146, s. 5, to be kept by the officiating minister in the manner provided by that Act, and, under 6 & 7 Will. IV, c. 86, the marriage registers are to be kept in duplicate, in books provided by the registrar-general. One copy is to be kept, with the registers of baptisms and burials, by the officiating minister.

for such preservation, and those orders shall be complied with by the parish council or parish meeting.

18.—*Parish wards.*—(1.) A county council may, on application by the parish council, or not less than one-tenth of the parochial electors of a parish, and on being satisfied that the area or population of the parish is so large, or different parts of the population so situated, as to make a single parish meeting for the election of councillors impracticable or inconvenient, or that it is desirable for any reason that certain parts of the parish should be separately represented on the council, order that the parish be divided for the purpose of electing parish councillors into wards, to be called parish wards, with such boundaries and such number of councillors for each ward as may be provided by the order.*

(2.) In the division of a parish into wards regard shall be had to the population according to the last published census for the time being, and to the evidence of any considerable change of population since that census, and to area, and to the distribution and pursuits of the population, and to all the circumstances of the case.

(3.) Any such order may be revoked or varied by the county council on application by either the council or not less than one-tenth of the parochial electors of the parish, but while in force shall have effect as if enacted by this Act.

(4.) In a parish divided into parish wards there

---

* This section will enable parishes consisting of several distinct communities to be fairly represented on the council. The constitution of the parish meetings for the several wards is provided for by s. 49.

shall be a separate election of parish councillors for each ward.

19.—*Provisions as to small parishes.*—In a rural parish not having a separate parish council, the following provisions shall, as from the appointed day, but subject to provisions made by a grouping order,* if the parish is grouped with some other parish or parishes, have effect—

> (1.) At the annual assembly the parish meeting shall choose a chairman for the year;†
> (2.) The parish meeting shall assemble not less than twice in each year;
> (3.) The parish meeting may appoint a committee of their own number for any purposes which, in the opinion of the parish meeting, would be better regulated and managed by means of such a committee, and all the acts of the committee shall be submitted to the parish meeting for their approval;
> (4.) All powers, duties, and liabilities of the vestry shall, except so far as they relate to the affairs of the church or to ecclesiastical charities, or are transferred by this Act to any other authority,‡ be transferred to the parish meeting;
> (5.) The power and the duty of appointing the overseers, and of notifying the appointment, and the power of appointing

---

* As to grouping orders, *see* s. 38.

† The "annual assembly" will take place at the time fixed by Sched. I, Part I (1).

‡ *i.e.* to the district council under s. 25.

and revoking the appointment of an assistant overseer, shall be transferred to and vest in the parish meeting, and the power given by this Act to a parish council of appointing trustees of a charity in the place of overseers or churchwardens, shall vest in the parish meeting;*

(6.) The chairman of the parish meeting and the overseers of the parish shall be a body corporate by the name of the chairman and overseers of the parish, and shall have perpetual succession, and may hold land for the purposes of the parish without licence in mortmain; but shall in all respects act in manner directed by the parish meeting, and any act of such body corporate shall be executed under the hands, or if an instrument under seal is required under the hands and seals, of the said chairman and overseers;

(7.) The legal interest in all property which under this Act would, if there were a parish council, be vested on the appointed day in the parish council† shall vest in the said body corporate of the chairman and overseers of the parish, subject to all trusts and liabilities affecting the same, and all persons concerned shall make or concur in making such transfers (if any) as are requisite to give effect to this enactment;

(8.) The provisions of this Act with respect to the stopping or diversion of a public right of way, or the declaring of a high-

---

* *See* ss. 5, 14. † *See* s. 5.

way to be unnecessary and not repairable at the public expense, and with respect to a complaint to a county council of a default by a district council,* shall apply, with the substitution of the parish meeting for the parish council;

(9.) A rate levied for defraying the expenses of the parish meeting (when added to expenses under any of the Adoptive Acts) shall not exceed sixpence in the pound in any local financial year;†

(10.) On the application of the parish meeting the county council may confer on that meeting any of the powers conferred on a parish council by this Act;

(11.) Any act of the parish meeting may be signified by an instrument executed at the meeting under the hands, or, if an instrument under seal is required under the hands and seals, of the chairman presiding at the meeting and two other parochial electors present at the meeting.

---

* The provisions referred to are ss. 13, 16. 26.

† This differs from s 11 (3), which applies to parishes under parish councils. In those cases the sums required for the Adoptive Acts can be raised *in addition* to 6d. in the £.

PART II.

Guardians and District Councils.

20.—*Election and qualification of guardians.*— As from the appointed day the following provisions shall apply to boards of guardians:—

(1.) There shall be no *ex-officio* or nominated guardians:

(2.) A person shall not be qualified to be elected or to be a guardian for a poor law union unless he is a parochial elector of some parish within the union, or has during the whole of the twelve months preceding the election resided in the union, or in the case of a guardian for a parish wholly or partly situate within the area of a borough, whether a county borough or not, is qualified to be elected a councillor for that borough, and no person shall be disqualified by sex or marriage for being elected or being a guardian.* So much of any enactment, whether in a public general or local and personal Act, as relates to the qualification of a guardian shall be repealed:

(3.) The parochial electors of a parish shall be the electors of the guardians for the parish, and, if the parish is divided into

---

* As to the qualifications of parochial electors *see* the Introduction, p. 20. The qualification for a town councillor is stated at p 64. As to disqualifications, *see* s. 46.

wards for the election of guardians, the electors of the guardians for each ward shall be such of the parochial electors as are registered in respect of qualifications within the ward :

(4.) Each elector may give one vote and no more for each of any number of persons not exceeding the number to be elected :

(5.) The election shall, subject to the provisions of this Act, be conducted according to rules framed under this Act by the Local Government Board :*

(6.) The term of office of a guardian shall be three years, and one-third, as nearly as may be, of every board of guardians shall go out of office on the fifteenth day of April in each year, and their places shall be filled by the newly elected guardians.† Provided as follows :—

(a) Where the county council on the application of the board of guardians of any union in their county consider that it would be expedient to provide for the simultaneous retirement of the whole of the board of guardians for the union, they may direct that the members of the board of guardians for that union shall retire together on the fifteenth day of April in every third year, and such order shall have full effect, and where a union is in more than one county, an order may be

---

* See s. 48.

† Where the mode of retirement is by one-third annually, the county council will arrange the rotation under s. 60,

made by a joint committee of the councils of those counties;

(b) Where at the passing of this Act the whole of the guardians of any union, in pursuance of an order of the Local Government Board, retire together at the end of every third year, they shall continue so to retire, unless the county council, or a joint committee of the county councils, on the application of the board of guardians or of any district council of a district wholly or partially within the union, otherwise direct:

(7.) A board of guardians may elect a chairman or vice-chairman, or both, and not more than two other persons, from outside their own body, but from persons qualified to be guardians of the union, and any person so elected shall be an additional guardian and member of the board. Provided that on the first election, if a sufficient number of persons who have been *ex-officio* or nominated guardians, of the union, and have actually served as such, are willing to serve, the additional members shall be elected from among those persons.*

21.—*Names of county districts and district councils.*—As from the appointed day,—

(1.) Urban sanitary authorities shall be called

---

* Note that it is only on the first election that such persons are entitled to preference.

urban district councils, and their districts shall be called urban districts; but nothing in this section shall alter the style or title of the corporation or council of a borough:

(2.) For every rural sanitary district there shall be a rural district council whose district shall be called a rural district:

(3.) In this and every other Act of Parliament, unless the context otherwise requires, the expression "district council" shall include the council of every urban district, whether a borough or not, and of every rural district, and the expression "county district" shall include every urban and rural district whether a borough or not.

22.—*Chairman of council to be justice.*—The chairman of a district council unless a woman or personally disqualified by any Act shall be by virtue of his office justice of the peace for the county in which the district is situate, but before acting as such justice he shall, if he has not already done so, take the oaths required by law to be taken by a justice of the peace other than the oath respecting the qualification by estate.*

23.—*Constitution of district councils in urban districts not being boroughs.*—As from the appointed day, where an urban district is not a borough—

---

* The mayor of a borough is by virtue of his office a justice for the borough, and this section places the chairman of a district council in the corresponding position of a justice for the county. It makes the mayor of a non-county borough a justice for the county as well as for the borough.

(1.) There shall be no *ex-officio* or nominated members of the urban sanitary authority:

(2.) A person shall not be qualified to be elected or to be a councillor unless he is a parochial elector of some parish within the district, or has during the whole of the twelve months preceding the election resided in the district, and no person shall be disqualified by sex or marriage for being elected or being a councillor.* So much of any enactment whether in a public general or local and personal Act as relates to the qualification of a member of an urban sanitary authority shall be repealed:

(3.) The parochial electors of the parishes in the district shall be the electors of the councillors of the district, and, if the district is divided into wards, the electors of the councillors for each ward shall be such of the parochial electors as are registered in respect of qualifications within the ward:

(4.) Each elector may give one vote and no more for each of any number of persons not exceeding the number to be elected:

(5.) The election shall, subject to the provisions of this Act, be conducted according to rules framed under this Act by the Local Government Board:†

(6.) The term of office of a councillor shall be three years, and one-third, as nearly as

---

* As to who are parochial electors and as to disqualifications, see respectively the Introduction (p. 20) and s. 46.

† *See* s. 48.

may be, of the council, and if the district is divided into wards one-third, as nearly as may be, of the councillors for each ward, shall go out of office on the fifteenth day of April in each year, and their places shall be filled by the newly elected councillors. Provided that a county council may on request made by a resolution of an urban district council, passed by two-thirds of the members voting on the resolution, direct that the members of such council shall retire together on the fifteenth day of April in every third year, and such order shall have full effect.

24.—*Rural district councils.*—(1.) The district council of every rural district shall consist of a chairman and councillors, and the councillors shall be elected by the parishes or other areas for the election of guardians in the district.

(2.) The number of councillors for each parish or other area in a rural district shall be the same as the number of guardians for that parish or area.

(3.) The district councillors for any parish or other area in a rural district shall be the representatives of that parish or area on the board of guardians, and when acting in that capacity shall be deemed to be guardians of the poor, and guardians as such shall not be elected for that parish or area.

(4.) The provisions of this Act with respect to the qualification, election, and term of office and retirement of guardians, and to the qualification of the chairman of the board of guardians,* shall

---

* *See* ss. 20, 59, 60.

apply to district councillors and to the chairman of the district council of a rural district, and any person qualified to be a guardian for a union comprising the district shall be qualified to be a district councillor for the district.

(5.) Where a rural sanitary district is on the appointed day situate in more than one administrative county, such portion thereof as is situate in each administrative county shall, save as otherwise provided by or in pursuance of this or any other Act,* be as from the appointed day a rural district;

Provided that where the number of councillors of any such district will be less than five, the provisions, so far as unrepealed,† of section nine of the Public Health Act, 1875, with respect to the nomination of persons to make up the members of a rural authority to five, shall apply, unless the Local Government Board by order direct that the affairs of the district shall be temporarily administered by the district council of an adjoining district in another county with which it was united before the appointed day, and, if they so direct, the councillors of the district shall be entitled, so far as regards those affairs, to sit and act as members of that district council, but a separate account shall be kept of receipts and expenses in respect of the district, and the same shall be credited or charged separately to the district.

(6.) The said provisions of section nine of the Public Health Act, 1875, shall apply to the district

* *See* s. 36 of this Act, and s. 57 of the Local Government Act, 1888, which will be found in the Appendix.

† The part repealed required persons nominated to have a certain qualification. These nominees will not be entitled to act as guardians (38 & 39 Vict. c. 55, s. 9).

council of a rural district to which they apply at the passing of this Act.

(7.) Every district council for a rural district shall be a body corporate by the name of the district council, with the addition of the name of the district, or if there is any doubt as to the latter name,[*] of such name as the county council direct, and shall have perpetual succession and a common seal, and may hold land for the purposes of their powers and duties without licence in mortmain.

25.—*Powers of district council with respect to sanitary and highway matters.*—(1.) As from the appointed day, there shall be transferred to the district council of every rural district all the powers, duties, and liabilities of the rural sanitary authority in the district, and of any highway authority in the district,[†] and highway boards shall cease to exist, and rural district councils shall be the successors of the rural sanitary authority and highway authority, and shall also have as respects highways all the powers, duties, and liabilities of an urban sanitary authority under sections one hundred and forty-four to one hundred and forty-eight of the Public Health Act, 1875,[‡] and those sections shall apply in the case of a rural district and of the council thereof in like manner as in the case of an urban district and an

---

[*] There would be doubt where a rural sanitary district was divided under subsection (5).

[†] "Highway authority" includes a highway board, or authority having the powers of a highway board, and the surveyors of highways or other officers performing similar duties (Local Government Act, 1888, s. 100; Local Government Act, 1894, s 75).

[‡] For the effect of these sections, *see* p. 78 of the Introduction.

urban authority. Provided that the council of any county may by order postpone within their county or any part thereof the operation of this section, so far as it relates to highways, for a term not exceeding three years from the appointed day or such further period as the Local Government Board may on the application of such council allow.*

(2.) Where a highway repairable ratione tenuræ appears on the report of a competent surveyor not to be in proper repair, and the person liable to repair the same fails when requested so to do by the district council to place it in proper repair, the district council may place the highway in proper repair, and recover from the person liable to repair the highway the necessary expenses of so doing.

(3.) Where a highway authority receives any contribution from the county council towards the cost of any highway under section eleven, subsection (10), of the Local Government Act, 1888,† such contribution may be made, subject to any such conditions for the proper maintenance and repair of such highways, as may be agreed on between the county council and the highway authority.

(4.) Where the council of a rural district become the highway authority for that district, any excluded part of a parish under section two hundred and sixteen of the Public Health Act, 1875, which is situate in that district, shall cease to be part of any

* The order is to make provision for holding elections of highway boards during the time for which the operation of the section is postponed, s. 84 (4).

† The county council are empowered to contribute towards the costs of the maintenance, repair, enlargement, and improvement of any highway in the county.

urban district for the purpose of highways, but until the council become the highway authority such excluded part of a parish shall continue subject to the said section.*

(5.) Rural district councils shall also have such powers, duties, and liabilities of urban sanitary authorities under the Public Health Acts or any other Act, and such provisions of any of those Acts relating to urban districts shall apply to rural districts, as the Local Government Board by general order direct.

(6.) The power to make such general orders shall be in addition to and not in substitution for the powers conferred on the Board by section two hundred and seventy-six of the Public Health Act, 1875, or by any enactment applying that section; and every order made by the Local Government Board under this section shall be forthwith laid before Parliament.

(7.) The powers conferred on the Local Government Board by the said section two hundred and seventy-six, or by any enactment applying that section, may be exercised on the application of a county council, or with respect to any parish or part of a parish on the application of the parish council of that parish.

26.—*Duties and powers of district council as to rights of way, rights of common, and roadside wastes.*—(1.) It shall be the duty of every district

---

* Under the section referred to, the whole of a parish only partly within an urban district for sanitary purposes may be wholly within that district for highway purposes. The part outside the district will, under this clause, be placed for the last-mentioned purposes under the rural district council, unless the operation of the clause is postponed under subsection (1).

council to protect all public rights of way, and to prevent as far as possible the stopping or obstruction of any such right of way, whether within their district or in an adjoining district in the county or counties in which the district is situate, where the stoppage or obstruction thereof would in their opinion be prejudicial to the interests of their district, and to prevent any unlawful encroachment on any roadside waste within their district.

(2.) A district council may with the consent of the county council for the county within which any common land is situate aid persons in maintaining rights of common where, in the opinion of the council, the extinction of such rights would be prejudicial to the inhabitants of the district; and may with the like consent exercise in relation to any common within their district all such powers as may, under section eight of the Commons Act, 1876, be exercised by an urban sanitary authority in relation to any common referred to in that section;* and notice of any application to the Board of Agriculture in relation to any common within their district shall be served upon the district council.

(3.) A district council may, for the purpose of carrying into effect this section, institute or defend any legal proceedings, and generally take such steps as they deem expedient.

(4.) Where a parish council have represented to the district council that any public right of way within the district or an adjoining district in the county or counties in which the district is situate has been unlawfully stopped or obstructed, or that an unlawful encroachment has taken place on any

---

* The effect of this is briefly stated in the Introduction, p. 80.

roadside waste within the district, it shall be the duty of the district council, unless satisfied that the allegations of such representation are incorrect, to take proper proceedings accordingly ; and if the district council refuse or fail to take any proceedings in consequence of such representation, the parish council may petition the county council for the county within which the way or waste is situate, and if that council so resolve the powers and duties of the district council under this section shall be transferred to the county council.*

(5.) Any proceedings or steps taken by a district council or county council in relation to any alleged right of way shall not be deemed to be unauthorised by reason only of such right of way not being found to exist.

(6.) Nothing in this section shall affect the powers of the county council in relation to roadside wastes.†

(7.) Nothing in this section shall prejudice any powers exerciseable by an urban sanitary authority at the passing of this Act, and the council of every county borough shall have the additional powers conferred on a district council by this section.

27.—*Transfer of certain powers of justices to district councils.*‡—(1.) As from the appointed day the powers, duties, and liabilities of justices out of session in relation to any of the matters following, that is to say,—

(*a*) the licensing of gang masters ;

* In connection with this subsection see s 63.
† See s 11 of the Local Government Act, 1888.
‡ See the reference to this clause at p. 80 of the Introduction.

(b) the grant of pawnbrokers' certificates;
(c) the licensing of dealers in game;
(d) the grant of licences for passage brokers and emigrant runners;
(e) the abolition of fairs and alteration of days for holding fairs;
(f) the execution as the local authority of the Acts relating to petroleum and infant life protection;

when arising within a county district, shall be transferred to the district council of the district.

(2.) As from the appointed day, the powers, duties, and liabilities of quarter sessions in relation to the licensing of knackers' yards within a county district shall be transferred to the district council of the district.

(3.) All fees payable in respect of the powers, duties, and liabilities transferred by this section shall be payable to the district council.

28.—*Expenses of urban district council.*—The expenses incurred by the council of an urban district in the execution of the additional powers conferred on the council by this Act shall, subject to the provisions of this Act, be defrayed in a borough out of the borough fund or rate, and in any other case out of the district fund and general district rate or other fund applicable towards defraying the expenses of the execution of the Public Health Act, 1875.*

29.—*Expenses of rural district council.*—The expenses incurred by the council of a rural district shall, subject to the provisions of this Act,

---

* The reference is to s. 207 of the Public Health Act, 1875.

be defrayed in manner directed by the Public Health Act, 1875, with respect to expenses incurred in the execution of that Act by a rural sanitary authority, and the provisions of the Public Health Acts with respect to those expenses shall apply accordingly.

Provided as follows :—

(a) Any highway expenses shall be defrayed as general expenses :

(b) When the Local Government Board determine any expenses under this Act to be special expenses and a separate charge on any contributory place, and such expenses would if not separately chargeable on a contributory place be raised as general expenses, they may further direct that such special expenses shall be raised in like manner as general expenses, and not by such separate rate for special expenses as is mentioned in section two hundred and thirty of the Public Health Act, 1875 :*

(c) A district council shall have the same power of charging highway expenses under exceptional circumstances on a contributory place as a highway board has in respect of any area under section seven of the Highways and Locomotives (Amendment) Act, 1878 :†

* "Special expenses" are a separate charge on each parish or other contributory place in the district. They are defrayed usually out of a separate rate to which occupiers of land are assessed at one-fourth. The effect of proviso (b) will be that in the cases mentioned, the special expenses will be leviable as poor rate, by an equal assessment of all occupiers of property in the contributory place.

† This will enable the district council, with the approval of

(d) Where highway expenses would, if this Act had not passed, have been in whole or in part defrayed in any parish or other area out of any property or funds other than rates, the district council shall make such provision as will give to that parish or area the benefit of such property or funds by way of reduction of the rates on the parish or area.

30.—*Guardians in London and county boroughs.*—The provisions of this Part of this Act respecting guardians shall apply to the administrative county of London and to every county borough.

31.—*Provisions as to London vestries and district boards.*—(1.) The provisions of this Act with respect to the qualification of the electors of urban district councillors, and of the persons to be elected, and with respect to the mode of conducting the election, shall apply as if members of the local board of Woolwich and the vestries elected under the Metropolis Management Acts, 1855 to 1890, or any Act amending those Acts, and the auditors for parishes elected under those Acts, and so far as respects the qualification of persons to be elected as if members of the district boards under the said Acts, were urban district councillors, and no person shall, *ex officio*, be chairman of any of the said vestries. Provided that the Elections (Hours of Poll) Act, 1885, shall apply to elections to the said vestries.*

the county council, to charge exclusively on one contributory place the cost of the highways in that place, if there are natural differences of soil or other exceptional circumstances.

* 48 Vict. c. 10. This Act requires the poll (if any) to be kept open from 8 o'clock in the morning till 8 o'clock at night.

(2.) Each of the said vestries, except those electing district boards, and each of the said district boards and the local board of Woolwich, shall at their first meeting after the annual election of members elect a chairman for the year, and section forty-one of the Metropolis Management Act, 1855,* shall apply only in case of the absence of such chairman, and the provisions of this Act with respect to chairmen of urban district councils being justices shall apply as if the said vestries and boards were urban district councils.†

(3.) Nothing in any local and personal Act shall prevent any vestry in the county of London from holding their meeting at such time as may be directed by the vestry.‡

32.—*Application to county boroughs of provisions as to transfer of justices' powers.*—The provisions of this Part of this Act respecting the powers, duties, and liabilities of justices out of session, or of quarter sessions, which are transferred to a district council, shall apply to a county borough as if it were an urban district, and the county borough council were a district council.§

33.—*Power to apply certain provisions of Act to urban districts and London.*—(1.) The Local Government Board may, on the application of the council

---

* (18 & 19 Vict. c. 120.) This section provides for the election of a chairman at each meeting of a district board.

† *See* s. 22.

‡ This was inserted to meet the case of one or more parishes in London where the vestry under the Metropolis Management Acts are prevented by local Acts from holding their meetings in the evening.

§ *See* s. 27.

of any municipal borough, including a county borough, or of any other urban district, make an order conferring on that council or some other representative body within the borough or district all or any of the following matters, namely, the appointment of overseers and assistant overseers, the revocation of appointment of assistant overseers, any powers, duties, or liabilities of overseers, and any powers, duties, or liabilities of a parish council, and applying with the necessary modifications the provisions of this Act with reference thereto.*

(2.) Where it appears to the Local Government Board that, by reason of the circumstances connected with any parish in a municipal borough (including a county borough) or other urban district divided into wards, or with the parochial charities of that parish, the parish will not, if the majority of the body of trustees administering the charity are appointed by the council of the borough or district, be properly represented on that body, they may, by their order, provide that such of those trustees as are appointed by the council, or some of them, shall be appointed on the nomination of the councillors elected for the ward or wards comprising such parish or any part of the parish.

(3) Any order under this section may provide for its operation extending either to the whole or to specified parts of the area of the borough or urban district, and may make such provisions as seem necessary for carrying the order into effect.

(4.) The order shall not alter the incidence of any rate, and shall make such provisions as may

---

* In connection with this provision *see* section 34.

seem necessary and just for the preservation of the existing interests of paid officers.

(5.) An order under this section may also be made on the application of any representative body within a borough or district.

(6.) The provisions of this section respecting councils of urban districts shall apply to the administrative county of London in like manner as if the district of each sanitary authority in that county were an urban district, and the sanitary authority were the council of that district.

(7.) The Local Government Board shall consult the Charity Commissioners before making any order under this section with respect to any charity.

34.—*Supplemental provisions as to control of overseers in urban districts.*—Where an order of the Local Government Board under this Act confers on the council of an urban district, or some other representative body within the district, either the appointment of overseers and assistant overseers, or the powers, duties, and liabilities of overseers, that order or any subsequent order of the Board may confer on such council or body the powers of the vestry under the third and fourth sections of the Poor Rate Assessment and Collection Act, 1869.*

35.—*Restrictions on application of Act to London, &c.*—Save as specially provided by this Act, this Part of this Act shall not apply to the administrative county of London or to a county borough.

* (32 & 33 Vict. c. 41.) The powers in question relate to the compounding of owners for rates. S. 4 provides for the compulsory rating of owners instead of occupiers.

PART III.

Areas and Boundaries.

36.—*Duties and powers of county council with respect to areas and boundaries.*—(1.) For the purpose of carrying this Act into effect in the case of—

- (*a*) every parish and rural sanitary district which at the passing of this Act is situate partly within and partly without an administrative county;* and
- (*b*) every parish which at the passing of this Act is situate partly within and partly without a sanitary district; and
- (*c*) every rural parish which has a population of less than two hundred;† and
- (*d*) every rural sanitary district which at the passing of this Act has less than five elective guardians capable of acting and voting as members of the rural sanitary authority of the district; and
- (*e*) every rural parish which is co-extensive with a rural sanitary district;

every county council shall forthwith take into consideration every such case within their county,

---

* A joint committee of the county councils concerned will act in these cases (subsection (11).)

† Surely this should have been 300 (*see* s. 1). The Government would appear to have accepted the final amendments of the House of Lords without making the necessary consequential amendments.

and whether any proposal has or has not been made as mentioned in section fifty-seven of the Local Government Act, 1888,* shall as soon as practicable, in accordance with that section, cause inquiries to be made and notices given, and make such orders, if any, as they deem most suitable for carrying into effect this Act in accordance with the following provisions, namely :—

> (i.) the whole of each parish, and, unless the county council for special reasons otherwise direct, the whole of each rural district shall be within the same administrative county;
>
> (ii.) the whole of each parish shall, unless the county council for special reasons otherwise direct, be within the same county district; and
>
> (iii.) every rural district which will have less than five elected councillors shall, unless for special reasons the county council otherwise direct, be united to some neighbouring district or districts.

(2.) Where a parish is at the passing of this Act situate in more than one urban district, the parts of the parish in each such district shall, as from the appointed day, unless the county council for special reasons otherwise direct, and subject to any alteration of area made by or in pursuance of this or any other Act, be separate parishes, in like manner as if they had been constituted separate parishes under the Divided Parishes and Poor Law Amendment Act, 1876, and the Acts amending the same.†

---

* This section will be found in the Appendix.

† They will, therefore, be separate parishes for practically all

(3.) Where a parish is divided by this Act, the county council may by order provide for the application to different parts of that parish of the provisions of this Act with respect to the appointment of trustees or beneficiaries of a charity* and for the custody of parish documents, but the order, so far as regards the charity, shall not have any effect until it has received the approval of the Charity Commissioners.

(4.) Where a rural parish is co-extensive with a rural sanitary district, then, until the district is united to some other district or districts, and unless the county council otherwise direct, a separate election of a parish council shall not be held for the parish, but the district council shall, in addition to their own powers, have the powers of, and be deemed to be, the parish council.

(5.) Where an alteration of the boundary of any county or borough seems expedient for any of the purposes mentioned in this section, application shall be made to the Local Government Board for an order under section fifty-four of the Local Government Act, 1888.†

(6.) Where the alteration of a poor law union seems expedient by reason of any of the provisions of this Act, the county council may, by their order, provide for such alteration in accordance with section fifty-eight† of the Local Government Act, 1888, or otherwise, but this provision shall not affect the powers of the Local Government Board with respect to the alteration of unions.

civil purposes, including the appointment of overseers. As to charities and the custody of documents in such cases, *see* subsection (3) of this section, and as to overseers and existing officers, sections 79 (11), 81. * *See* s. 14.

† This section will be found in the Appendix.

(7.) Where an order for the alteration of the boundary of any parish or the division thereof, or the union thereof or of any part thereof, with another parish is proposed to be made after the appointed day, notice thereof shall, a reasonable time before it is made, be given to the parish council of that parish, or if there is no parish council, to the parish meeting, and that parish council or parish meeting, as the case may be, shall have the right to appear at any inquiry held by the county council with reference to the order, and shall be at liberty to petition the Local Government Board against the confirmation of the order.

(8.) Where the alteration of the boundary of any parish, or the division thereof or the union thereof or of part thereof with another parish, seems expedient for any of the purposes of this Act, provision for such alteration, division, or union may be made by an order of the county council confirmed by the Local Government Board under section fifty-seven of the Local Government Act, 1888.*

(9.) Where a parish is by this Act divided into two or more parishes, those parishes shall, until it is otherwise provided, be included in the same poor law union in which the original parish was included.

(10.) Subject to the provisions of this Act, any order made by a county council in pursuance of this Part of this Act shall be deemed to be an order under section fifty-seven* of the Local Government Act, 1888, and any board of guardians affected by an order shall have the same right of petitioning

* This section will be found in the Appendix.

against that order as is given by that section to any other authority.*

(11.) Where any of the areas referred to in section fifty-seven of the Local Government Act, 1888, is situate in two or more counties, or the alteration of any such area would alter the boundaries of a poor law union situate in two or more counties, a joint committee appointed by the councils of those counties shall, subject to the terms of delegation, be deemed to have and to have always had power to make orders under that section with respect to that area;† and where at the passing of this Act a rural sanitary district or parish is situate in more than one county, a joint committee of the councils of those counties shall act under this section, and if any of those councils do not, within two months after request from any other of them, appoint members of such joint committee, the members of the committee actually appointed shall act as the joint committee. Provided that any question arising as to the constitution or procedure of any such joint committee shall, if the county councils concerned fail to agree, be determined by the Local Government Board.

(12.) Every report made by the Boundary Commissioners under the Local Government Boundaries Act, 1887, shall be laid before the council of any administrative county or borough affected by that report, and before any joint committee of county councils, and it shall be the duty of such councils and joint committees to take such reports into

* In connection with this, the provisions of ss. 40-42, 80 (2), should be noticed.

† This is an amendment of the Act of 1888, and supplies a defect therein. As to the appointment of joint committees of county councils, see s. 81 of that Act.

consideration before framing any order under the powers conferred on them under this Act.*

(13.) Every county council shall, within two years after the passing of this Act, or within such further period as the Local Government Board may allow either generally or with reference to any particular matter, make such orders under this section as they deem necessary for the purpose of bringing this Act into operation, and after the expiration of the said two years or further period the powers of the county council for that purpose shall be transferred to the Local Government Board, who may exercise those powers.

37.—*Provision as to parishes having parts with defined boundaries.*—Where it is proved to the satisfaction of the county council that any part of a parish has a defined boundary, and has any property or rights distinct from the rest of the parish, the county council may order that the consent of a parish meeting held for that part of the parish† shall be required for any such act or class of acts of the parish council affecting the said property or rights as is specified in the order.‡

38.—*Orders for grouping parishes and dissolving groups.*—(1.) Where parishes are grouped, the grouping order shall make the necessary provisions for the name of the group, for the parish meetings

---

* (50 & 51 Vict. c. 61.) See a similar provision in s. 53 of the Act of 1888. The council or joint committee are not bound to give effect to the Commissioners' recommendations.

† See s. 49 as to such meetings.

‡ The parish meeting may, in such cases, require the parish council to appoint a committee to exercise their powers and duties affecting the part of the parish in question (s. 56).

in each of the grouped parishes, and for the election in manner provided by this Act of separate representatives of each parish on the parish council, and may provide for the consent of the parish meeting of a parish to any particular act of the parish council, and for any other adaptations of this Act to the group of parishes, or to the parish meetings in the group.

(2.) Where parishes are grouped the whole area under each parish council shall, unless the county council for special reasons otherwise direct, be within the same administrative county and county district.

(3.) Where parishes are grouped, the grouping order shall provide for the application of the provisions of this Act with respect to the appointment of trustees and beneficiaries of a charity, and the custody of documents, so as to preserve the separate rights of each parish.*

(4.) The parish meeting of any parish may apply to the county council for a grouping order respecting that parish, and, if the parish has a less population than two hundred,† for a parish council, and any such application shall be forthwith taken into consideration by the county council.

(5.) The county council may, on the application of the council for any group of parishes or of the parish meeting for any parish included in a group of parishes, make an order dissolving the group, and shall by the order make such provision as appears necessary for the election of parish councils of the parishes in the group and for the adjustment of property, rights, and liabilities as between separate parishes and the group.

* *See* ss. 14, 17. † *See* note p. 165.

39.—*Provisions for increase and decrease of population.*—(1.) Where the population of a parish not having a separate parish council increases so as to justify the election of such council, the parish meeting may petition the county council, and the county council, if they think proper, may order the election of a parish council in that parish, and shall by the order make such provision as appears necessary for separating the parish from any group of parishes in which it is included, and for the alteration of the parish council of the group, and for the adjustment of property, rights, and liabilities as between the group and the parish with a separate parish council.

(2.) Where the population of a parish, according to the last published census for the time being is less than two hundred,* the parish meeting may petition the county council, and the county council, if they think proper, may order the dissolution of the parish council, and from and after the date of the order this Act shall apply to that parish as to a parish not having a parish council.† The order shall make such provision as appears necessary for carrying it into effect, and for the disposal and adjustment of the property, rights, and liabilities of the parish council. Where a petition for such an order is rejected, another petition for the same purpose may not be presented within two years from the presentation of the previous petition.

40.—*Certain orders of county council not to require confirmation.*—A grouping order, and an order establishing or dissolving a parish council, or dissolving a group of parishes, and an order relating to the

---

* *See* note p. 165. † The reference is to s. 19.

custody of parish documents or requiring the approval of the Charity Commissioners, and an order requiring the consent of the parish meeting for any part of the parish to any act or class of acts of the parish council,* shall not require submission to or confirmation by the Local Government Board.

41.—*Reduction of time for appealing against county council orders.*—The time for petitioning against an order under section fifty-seven of the Local Government Act, 1888,† shall be six weeks instead of three months after the notice referred to in subsection three of that section.

42.—*Validity of county council orders.*—When an order under section fifty-seven of the Local Government Act, 1888,† has been confirmed by the Local Government Board, such order shall at the expiration of six months from that confirmation be presumed to have been duly made, and to be within the powers of that section, and no objection to the legality thereof shall be entertained in any legal proceeding whatever.

* This relates to orders such as may be made under ss. 1 (1), 17 (9), 36 (3), 37-39.
† *See* this section in the Appendix.

PART IV.

SUPPLEMENTAL.

Parish Meetings and Elections.

43.—*Removal of disqualification of married women.*—For the purposes of this Act a woman shall not be disqualified by marriage for being on any local government register of electors, or for being an elector of any local authority, provided that a husband and wife shall not both be qualified in respect of the same property.

44.—*Register of parochial electors.**—(1.) The local government register of electors and the parliamentary register of electors, so far as they relate to a parish shall, together, form the register of the parochial electors of the parish; and any person whose name is not in that register shall not be entitled to attend a meeting or vote as a parochial elector, and any person whose name is in

---

* The effect of this clause in its technical aspect could hardly be made plain to the ordinary reader without a more lengthy description than we can permit ourselves. The principal points are that a person may be registered, if duly qualified, in more than one register of parochial electors; that no person who is not on the register of parochial electors can take part in parish meetings or vote as parochial elector, and that a person, duly qualified, may claim to be put on the separate list of parochial electors referred to in the section. Ownership voters in a parish within a parliamentary borough are enabled to vote as parochial electors of that parish by subsection (2).

that register shall be entitled to attend a meeting and vote as a parochial elector unless prohibited from voting by this or any other Act of Parliament.

(2.) Where the parish is in a parliamentary borough, such portion of the parliamentary register of electors for the county as contains the names of persons registered in respect of the ownership of any property in the parish shall be deemed to form part of the parliamentary register of electors for the parish within the meaning of this section.

(3.) The lists and register of electors in any parish shall be framed in parts for wards of urban districts and parishes in such manner that they may be conveniently used as lists for polling at elections for any such wards.

(4.) Nothing in any Act shall prevent a person, if duly qualified, from being registered in more than one register of parochial electors.

(5.) Where in that portion of the parliamentary register of electors which relates to a parish a person is entered to vote in a polling district other than the district comprising the parish, such person shall be entitled to vote as a parochial elector for that parish, and in addition to an asterisk there shall be placed against his name a number consecutive with the other numbers in the list.

(6.) Where the revising barrister in any list of voters for a parish would—

> (a) In pursuance of section seven of the County Electors Act, 1888,* place an asterisk or other mark against the name of any person; or

* 51 Vict. c. 10.

(*b*) In pursuance of section four of the Registration Act, 1885, erase the name of any person otherwise than by reason of that name appearing more than once in the lists for the same parish; or

(*c*) in pursuance of section twenty-eight of the Parliamentary and Municipal Registration Act, 1878,* as amended by section five of the Registration Act, 1885,† place against the name of a person a note to the effect that such person is not entitled to vote in respect of the qualification contained in the list,

the revising barrister shall, instead of placing that mark or note, or erasing the name, place against the name, if the person is entitled to vote in respect of that entry as a county elector or burgess, a mark signifying that his name should be printed in division three of the list,‡ or if he is entitled to vote only as a parochial elector, a mark signifying that he is entitled to be registered as a parochial elector, and the name so marked shall not be printed in the parliamentary register of electors, but shall be printed, as the case requires, either in division three of the local government register of electors, or in a separate list of parochial electors.

(7.) Where the name of a person is entered both in the ownership list and in the occupation list of voters in the same parish, and the revising barrister places against that name a mark or note signifying that the name should be printed in

---

* 41 & 42 Vict. c. 26.   † 48 & 49 Vict. c. 15.

‡ Division 3 of the Occupiers' List contains the names of persons entitled to be registered as county electors or burgesses, but not as parliamentary voters

division three of the lists, an asterisk or other mark shall be there printed against the name, and such person shall not be entitled to vote as a parochial elector in respect of that entry.

(8.) Such separate list shall form part of the register of parochial electors of the parish, and shall be printed at the end of the other lists of electors for the parish, and the names shall be numbered consecutively with the other names on those lists, and the law relating to the register of electors shall, with the necessary modifications, apply accordingly, and the lists shall, for the purposes of this Act, be deemed to be part of such register.

(9.) Any person may claim for the purpose of having his name entered in the parochial electors' list, and the law relating to claims to be entered in lists of voters shall apply.

(10.) The clerk of the county council or town clerk, as the case may be, shall, in printing the lists returned to him by the revising barrister, do everything that is necessary for carrying into effect the provisions of this section with respect to the persons whose names are marked by the revising barrister in pursuance of this section.

45.—*Supplemental provisions as to parish meetings.*—(1.) Subject to the provisions of this Act, parish meetings shall be held on such days and at such times and places as may be fixed by the parish council, or, if there is no parish council, by the chairman of the parish meeting.*

(2.) If the chairman of the parish council is

---

* The words "subject to the provisions of this Act" have reference to sections 2 (3), 19 (2), Sched. I, Part I (1).

present at a parish meeting and is not a candidate for election at the meeting, he shall, save as otherwise provided by this Act, be the chairman of the meeting.*

(3.) The chairman of the parish council, or any two parish councillors, or the chairman of the parish meeting, or any six parochial electors, may at any time convene a parish meeting.†

46.—*Disqualifications for parish or district council.*—(1.) A person shall be disqualified for being elected or being a member or chairman of a council of a parish or of a district other than a borough or of a board of guardians if he—

- (*a*) is an infant or an alien ; or
- (*b*) has within twelve months before his election, or since his election, received union or parochial relief ; or
- (*c*) has, within five years before his election or since his election, been convicted either on indictment or summarily of any crime, and sentenced to imprisonment with hard labour without the option of a fine, or to any greater punishment, and has not received a free pardon, or has, within or during the time aforesaid, been adjudged bankrupt, or made a composition or arrangement with his creditors ; or
- (*d*) holds any paid office under the parish

---

* If the chairman of the parish council is absent, or is unable or unwilling to take the chair, the meeting will elect a chairman (Sched. I, Part I (10).)

† As to the mode of convening parish meetings, *see* s. 51 and Sched. I, Part I.

council or district council or board of guardians, as the case may be; or

(e) is concerned in any bargain or contract entered into with the council or board, or participates in the profit of any such bargain or contract or of any work done under the authority of the council or board.

(2.) Provided that a person shall not be disqualified for being elected or being a member or chairman of any such council or board by reason of being interested—

(a) in the sale or lease of any lands or in any loan of money to the council or board, or in any contract with the council for the supply from land, of which he is owner or occupier, of stone, gravel, or other materials for making or repairing high- materials for the repair of roads or ways or bridges, or in the transport of bridges in his own immediate neighbourhood; or

(b) in any newspaper in which any advertisement relating to the affairs of the council or board is inserted; or

(c) in any contract with the council or board as a shareholder in any joint stock company; but he shall not vote at any meeting of the council or board on any question in which such company are interested, except that in the case of a water company or other company established for the carrying on of works of a like public nature, this prohibition may be dispensed with by the county council.

(3.) Where a person who is a parish councillor, or is a candidate for election as a parish councillor, is concerned in any such bargain or contract, or participates in any such profit, as would disqualify him for being a parish councillor, the disqualification may be removed by the county council if they are of opinion that such removal will be beneficial to the parish.

(4.) Where a person is disqualified by being adjudged bankrupt or making a composition or arrangement with his creditors, the disqualification shall cease, in case of bankruptcy, when the adjudication is annulled, or when he obtains his discharge with a certificate that his bankruptcy was caused by misfortune without any misconduct on his part, and, in case of composition or arrangement, on payment of his debts in full.

(5.) A person disqualified for being a guardian shall also be disqualified for being a rural district councillor.*

(6.) If a member of a council of a parish, or of a district other than a borough, or of a board of guardians, is absent from meetings of the council or board for more than six months consecutively, except in case of illness or for some reason approved by the council or board, his office shall on the expiration of those months become vacant.

(7.) Where a member of a council or board of guardians becomes disqualified for holding office, or vacates his seat for absence, the council or board shall forthwith declare the office to be vacant, and signify the same by notice signed by three members

* This almost necessarily follows from the provision that rural district councillors shall act as guardians for the parishes which they represent (s. 24 (3).)

and countersigned by the clerk of the council or board, and notified in such manner as the council or board direct, and the office shall thereupon become vacant.

(8.) If any person acts when disqualified, or votes when prohibited under this section, he shall for each offence be liable on summary conviction to a fine not exceeding twenty pounds.

(9.) This section shall apply in the case of any authority whose members are elected in accordance with this Act in like manner as if that authority were a district council, and in the case of London auditors as if they were members of a district council.

47.—*Supplemental provisions as to parish councils.*—(1.) If at the annual election of parish councillors any vacancies are not filled by election, such number of the retiring councillors as are not re-elected, and are required to fill the vacancies, shall, if willing, continue to hold office. The councillors so to continue shall be those who were highest on the poll at the previous election, or if the numbers were equal or there was no poll, as may be determined by the parish meeting, or if not so determined, by the chairman of the parish council.

(2.) A retiring parish councillor or chairman of a parish council or parish meeting shall be re-eligible.

(3.) A parish councillor may, by notice in writing to the chairman of the council, resign his office, and a chairman of a parish council or parish meeting may resign his chairmanship by notice in writing to the council or meeting.*

* The resignation of guardians, district councillors (other than borough councillors), and London vestrymen is provided for in 48 (4).

(4.) A casual vacancy among parish councillors or in the office of chairman of the council shall be filled by the parish council, and where there is no parish council, a casual vacancy in the office of chairman of the parish meeting shall be filled by the parish meeting, and the person elected shall retire from office at the time when the vacating councillor or chairman would have retired.

(5.) If any parish council become unable to act by reason of a want of councillors, whether from failure to elect or otherwise, the county council may order a new election, and may by order make such provision as seems expedient for authorising any person to act temporarily in the place of the parish council and of the chairman thereof.

48.—*Supplemental provisions as to elections, polls, and tenure of office.**—(1.) The election of a parish councillor shall be at a parish meeting, or at a poll consequent thereon.

(2.) Rules framed under this Act by the Local Government Board in relation to elections shall, notwithstanding anything in any other Act, have effect as if enacted in this Act, and shall provide, amongst other things—

(i.) for every candidate being nominated in writing by two parochial electors as proposer and seconder and no more;†

(ii.) for preventing an elector at an election for a union or for a district not a borough

---

* In connection with this section, *see* the "Introduction," pp. 90-94.

† In a borough, nominations are required to be subscribed by eight persons "assenting to the nomination," besides the proposer and seconder.

from subscribing a nomination paper or voting in more than one parish or other area in the union or district;

(iii.) for preventing an elector at an election for a parish divided into parish wards from subscribing a nomination paper or voting for more than one ward;

(iv.) for fixing or enabling the county council to fix the day of the poll and the hours during which the poll is to be kept open, so, however, that the poll shall always be open between the hours of six and eight in the evening;

(v.) for the polls at elections held at the same date and in the same area being taken together, except where this is impracticable;

(vi.) for the appointment of returning officers for the elections.

(3.) At every election regulated by rules framed under this Act, the poll shall be taken by ballot, and the Ballot Act, 1872,* and the Municipal Elections (Corrupt and Illegal Practices) Act, 1884,† and sections seventy-four and seventy-five and Part IV. of the Municipal Corporations Act, 1882,‡ as amended by the last-mentioned Act (including the penal provisions of those Acts) shall, subject to adaptations, alterations, and exceptions made by such rules, apply in like manner as in the case of a municipal election. Provided that—

(a) section six of the Ballot Act, 1872, shall apply in the case of such elections, and

---

* 35 & 36 Vict. c. 33. † 47 & 48 Vict. c. 70.
‡ 45 & 46 Vict. c. 50.

the returning officer may, in addition to using the schools and public rooms therein referred to free of charge, for taking the poll, use the same, free of charge, for hearing objections to nomination papers and for counting votes; and

(*b*) section thirty-seven of the Municipal Elections (Corrupt and Illegal Practices) Act, 1884, shall apply as if the election were an election mentioned in the First Schedule to that Act.*

(4.) The provisions of the Municipal Corporations Act, 1882, and the enactments amending the same, with respect to the expenses of elections of councillors of a borough, and to the acceptance of office, resignation, re-eligibility of holders of office, and the filling of casual vacancies, and section fifty-six of that Act, shall, subject to the adaptations, alterations, and exceptions made by the said rules, apply in the case of guardians and of district councillors of a county district not a borough, and of members of the local board of Woolwich, and of a vestry under the Metropolis Management Acts, 1855 to 1890, and any Act amending the same. Provided that—

* This makes certain provisions of the Municipal Elections (Corrupt and Illegal Practices) Act inapplicable to elections regulated by rules framed under the present Act, viz., those provisions which "prohibit the payment of any sum, and the incurring of any expense by, or on behalf of a candidate at an election, on account of, or in respect of, the conduct or management of the election, and those which relate to the time for sending in and paying claims, and those which relate to the maximum amount of election expenses, or the return or declaration respecting election expenses."

(*a*) the provisions as to resignation shall not apply to guardians, and district councillors of a rural district shall be in the same position with respect to resignation as members of a board of guardians ;* and

(*b*) nothing in the enactments applied by this section shall authorise or require a returning officer to hold an election to fill a casual vacancy which occurs within six months before the ordinary day of retirement from the office in which the vacancy occurs, and the vacancy shall be filled at the next ordinary election ;† and

(*c*) the rules may provide for the incidence of the charge for the expenses of the elections of guardians being the same as heretofore.

(5.) If any difficulty arises as respects the election of any individual councillor or guardian, or member of any such local board or vestry as aforesaid, or auditor, and there is no provision for holding another election, the county council may order a new election to be held and give such directions as may be necessary for the purpose of holding the election.

(6.) Any ballot boxes, fittings, and compartments provided by or belonging to any public authority, for any election (whether parliamentary, county council, municipal, school board, or other),

---

* *See* s. 47 (3), as to the resignation of parish councillors or of the chairman of the parish council or parish meeting.

† A similar provision is made as regards casual vacancies on county councils by s. 1 of the County Councils Election Act, 1891 (54 & 55 Vict, c. 68).

shall, on request, and if not required for immediate use by the said authority, be lent to the returning officer for an election under this Act, upon such conditions and either free of charge or, except in the prescribed cases, for such reasonable charge as may be prescribed.

(7.) The expenses of any election under this Act shall not exceed the scale fixed by the county council, and if at the beginning of one month before the first election under this Act a county council have not framed any such scale for their county, the Local Government Board may frame a scale for the county, and the scale so framed shall apply to the first election, and shall have effect as if it had been made by the county council, but shall not be alterable until after the first election.

(8.) This section shall, subject to any adaptations made by the said rules, apply in the case of every poll consequent on a parish meeting, as if it were a poll for the election of parish councillors.

49.—*Provision as to parish meeting for part of parish.*—Where a parish meeting is required or authorised in pursuance of this Act to be held for a ward or other part of a parish,* then—

> (a) the persons entitled to attend and vote at the meeting, or at any poll consequent thereon, shall be the parochial electors registered in respect of qualifications in that ward or part; and
>
> (b) the provisions of this Act with respect to parish meetings for the whole of a parish,

* Parish meetings for parts of parishes may be held under ss. 7 (4), 18, 37, 53 (1), 56 (2).

including the provisions with respect to the convening of a parish meeting by parochial electors, shall apply as if the ward or part were the whole parish.

50.—*Supplemental provisions as to overseers.*— If, in the case of a rural parish or of any urban parish in respect to which the power of appointing overseers has been transferred under this Act, notice in the prescribed form * of the appointment of overseers is not received by the guardians of the poor law union comprising the parish within three weeks after the fifteenth day of April,† or after the occurrence of a vacancy in the office of overseer, as the case may be, the guardians shall make the appointment or fill the vacancy, and any overseer appointed by the guardians shall supersede any overseer previously appointed whose appointment has not been notified. Any such notice shall be admissible as evidence that the appointment has been duly made.

Parish and District Councils.

51.—*Public notices.*—A public notice given by a parish council for the purposes of this Act, or otherwise for the execution of their duties, and a public notice of a parish meeting, shall be given in the manner required for giving notice of vestry meet-

---

* "Prescribed" means prescribed by order of the Local Government Board (s. 75).

† The first appointment of overseers by the parish council will take place in April, 1895. The appointment for the year 1894-5 were to be made by the justices as usual on, or within fourteen days after, the 25th March (54 Geo. III, c. 91).

ings,* and by posting the notice in some conspicuous place or places within the parish, and in such other manner (if any) as appears to the council or to the persons convening the meeting desirable for giving publicity to the notice.

52.—*Supplemental provisions as to transfer of powers.*—(1.) Any power which may be exercised and any consent which may be given by the owners and ratepayers of a parish or by the majority of them under any of the Acts relating to the relief of the poor or under the School Sites Acts or the Literary and Scientific Institutions Act, 1854, so far as respects the dealing with parish property or the spending of money or raising of a rate may, in the case of a rural parish, be exercised or given by the parish meeting of the parish.†

(2.) In a rural parish the power of making an application or passing a resolution given by section twelve of the Elementary Education Act, 1870,‡ and by section forty-one of the Elementary Education Act, 1876,§ to the electing body mentioned in the former section shall be transferred to the parish meeting of the parish, and shall in cases under the latter section be exerciseable by the like majority of the parish meeting,|| and, if a poll is taken, of the parochial electors, as

---

* *i.e.* by being posted at the doors of all the churches and chapels in the parish. As to the time for the publication of a notice of a parish meeting, see Sched. I, Part I (2) (3).

† *See* p. 27 of the Introduction.

‡ 33 & 34 Vict. c. 75.

§ 39 & 40 Vict. c. 79.

|| *i.e.* a two-thirds majority (39 & 40 Vict. c. 79, s. 41).

is required by that section in the case of the said electing body, and rule two of the Second Part of the Second Schedule to the former Act with respect to the passing of such resolutions shall not apply.*

(3.) The consent of justices shall not be required for the sale of land belonging to a parish which has been used for materials for the repair of highways or for the purchase of land with the proceeds of any such sale.†

(4.) Where the legal estate in any property is vested in the churchwardens and overseers of any parish by virtue of the Poor Relief Act, 1819,‡ nothing in the Charitable Trusts Acts, 1853 to 1891, shall be deemed to require the consent of such churchwardens and overseers in their capacity as a corporation under that Act, or of the parish council as their successors, to a vesting order under those Acts dealing with the said legal estate. Provided that nothing in this section shall affect any rights, powers, or duties of the churchwardens and overseers or the parish council, in cases where they have active powers of management.

(5.) All enactments in any Act, whether general or local and personal, relating to any powers,

---

* The rule referred to is to the effect that the resolution of the electing body shall be passed as nearly as possible in like manner as a school board is elected. The reference in this subsection is to an application for the formation or dissolution of a school board.

† See s. 48 of the Highway Act, 1835 (5 & 6 Will. IV, c. 50), under which land allotted to the parish for materials, when exhausted, may be sold and other land purchased, with consent of justices.

‡ 59 Geo. III, c. 12.

duties, or liabilities transferred by this Act to a parish council or parish meeting from justices or the vestry or overseers or churchwardens and overseers shall, subject to the provisions of this Act and so far as circumstances admit, be construed as if any reference therein to justices or to the vestry, or to the overseers, or to the churchwardens and overseers, referred to the parish council or parish meeting as the case requires, and the said enactments shall be construed with such modifications as may be necessary for carrying this Act into effect.

53.—*Supplemental provisions as to adoptive Acts.*—(1.) Where on the appointed day any of the adoptive Acts is in force in a part only of a rural parish, the existing authority under the Act, or the parish meeting for that part, may transfer the powers, duties, and liabilities of the authority to the parish council, subject to any conditions with respect to the execution thereof by means of a committee as to the authority or parish meeting may seem fit, and any such conditions may be altered by any such parish meeting.*

(2.) If the area on the appointed day under any authority under any of the adoptive Acts will not after that day be comprised within one rural parish, the powers and duties of the authority shall be transferred to the parish councils of the rural parishes wholly or partly comprised in that area, or, if the area is partly comprised in an urban district, to those parish councils and the district council of the urban district, and

---

* As to parish meetings for parts of parishes, *see* s. 49, and as to the appointment of committees, s. 56. The Adoptive Acts are defined by s. 7.

shall, until other provision is made in pursuance of this Act, be exercised by a joint committee* appointed by those councils. Where any such rural parish has not a parish council the parish meeting shall, for the purposes of this provision, be substituted for the parish council.

(3.) The property, debts, and liabilities of any authority under any of the adoptive Acts whose powers are transferred in pursuance of this Act shall continue to be the property, debts, and liabilities of the area of that authority, and the proceeds of the property shall be credited, and the debts and liabilities and the expenses incurred in respect of the said powers, duties, and liabilities, shall be charged to the account of the rates or contributions levied in that area, and where that area is situate in more than one parish the sums credited to and paid by each parish shall be apportioned in such manner as to give effect to this enactment.

(4.) The county council on the application of a parish council may, by order, alter the boundaries of any such area if they consider that the alteration can properly be made without any undue alteration of the incidence of liability to rates and contributions or of the right to property belonging to the area, regard being had to any corresponding advantage to persons subject to the liability or entitled to the right.

54.—*Effect on parish council of constitution of urban district.*—(1.) Where a new borough is created, or any other new urban district is constituted, or the area of an urban district is extended, then—

* With respect to joint committees, *see* s. 57.

(a) as respects any rural parish or part of a rural parish which will be comprised in the borough or urban district, provision shall be made, either by the constitution of a new parish, or by the annexation of the parish or parts thereof to another parish or parishes, or otherwise, for the appointment of overseers and for placing the parish or part in the same position as other parishes in the borough or district, and

(b) as respects any parish or part which remains rural, provision shall be made for the constitution of a new parish council for the same, or for the annexation of the parish or part to some other parish or parishes, or otherwise for the government of the parish or part, and

(c) provision shall also where necessary be made for the adjustment of any property, debts, and liabilities affected by the said creation, constitution, or extension.*

(2.) The provision aforesaid shall be made—

(a) Where a new borough is created, by a scheme under section two hundred and thirteen of the Municipal Corporations Act, 1882;

(b) Where any other new urban district is constituted, by an order of the county council under section fifty-seven of the Local Government Act, 1888;†

(c) Where the area of an urban district is

---

* Adjustments of property and liabilities under this Act are dealt with in s. 68. † *See* Appendix.

extended, by an order of the Local Government Board under section fifty-four, or of the county council under section fifty-seven, as the case may be, of the Local Government Act, 1888.*

(3.) Where the area of an urban district is diminished this section shall apply with the necessary modifications.

55.—*Power to change name of district or parish.*—(1.) Where a parish is divided or united or grouped with another parish by an order in pursuance of this Act each new parish or group so formed shall bear such name as the order directs.

(2.) Where a parish is divided by this Act, each parish so formed shall bear such name as the county council direct.

(3.) Any district council may, with the sanction of the county council, change their name and the name of their district.

(4.) Every change of name made in pursuance of this section shall be published in such manner as the authority authorising the change may direct, and shall be notified to the Local Government Board.

(5.) Any such change of name shall not affect any rights or obligations of any parish, district, council, authority, or person, or render defective any legal proceedings, and any legal proceedings may be continued or commenced as if there were no change of name.

56.—*Committees of parish or district councils.*—(1.) A parish or district council may appoint com-

* These sections will be found in the Appendix

mittees, consisting either wholly or partly of members of the council, for the exercise of any powers which, in the opinion of the council, can be properly exercised by committees, but a committee shall not hold office beyond the next annual meeting of the council, and the acts of every such committee shall be submitted to the council for their approval.

Provided that where a committee is appointed by any district council for any of the purposes of the Public Health Acts or Highway Acts, the council may authorise the committee to institute any proceeding or do any act which the council might have instituted or done for that purpose other than the raising of any loan or the making of any rate or contract.

(2.) Where a parish council have any powers and duties which are to be exercised in a part only of the parish, or in relation to a recreation ground, building, or property held for the benefit of a part of a parish, and the part has a defined boundary, the parish council shall, if required by a parish meeting held for that part,* appoint annually to exercise such powers and duties a committee consisting partly of members of the council and partly of other persons representing the said part of the parish.

(3.) With respect to committees of parish and district councils the provisions in the First Schedule to this Act shall have effect.

(4.) This section shall not apply to the council of a borough.†

* As to parish meetings for parts of parishes *see* s. 49.

† The appointment of committees by town councils of boroughs is provided for by s. 22 of the Municipal Corporations Act, 1882.

57.—*Joint committees.*—(1.) A parish or district council may concur with any other parish or district council or councils in appointing out of their respective bodies a joint committee for any purpose in respect of which they are jointly interested, and in conferring, with or without conditions or restrictions, on any such committee any powers which the appointing council might exercise if the purpose related exclusively to their own parish or district.

(2.) Provided that a council shall not delegate to any such committee any power to borrow money or make any rate.

(3.) A joint committee appointed under this section shall not hold office beyond the expiration of fourteen days after the next annual meeting of any of the councils who appointed it.

(4.) The costs of a joint committee under this section shall be defrayed by the councils by whom it is appointed in such proportions as they may agree upon, or as may be determined in case of difference by the county council.

(5.) Where a parish council can under this Act be required to appoint a committee consisting partly of members of the council and partly of other persons,* that requirement may also be made in the case of a joint committee, and shall be duly complied with by the parish councils concerned at the time of the appointment of such committee.

58.—*Audit of accounts of district and parish councils and inspection.*—(1.) The accounts of the receipts and payments of parish and district councils, and of parish meetings for parishes not having parish councils, and their committees and

* *See* section 56 (2)

officers, shall be made up yearly to the thirty-first day of March, or in the case of accounts which are required to be audited half-yearly,* then half-yearly to the thirtieth day of September and the thirty-first day of March in each year, and in such form as the Local Government Board prescribe.

(2.) The said accounts shall, except in the case of accounts audited by the auditors of a borough, (but inclusive of the accounts of a joint committee appointed by a borough council with another council not being a borough council,) be audited by a district auditor, and the enactments relating to audit by district auditors of accounts of urban sanitary authorities and their officers, and to all matters incidental thereto and consequential thereon,† shall apply accordingly, except that in the case of the accounts of rural district councils, their committees and officers, the audit shall be half-yearly instead of yearly.

(3.) The Local Government Board may, with respect to any audit to which this section applies, make rules modifying the enactments as to publication of notice of the audit and of the abstract of accounts and the report of the auditor.‡

* In the case of rural district councils there will be a half-yearly audit (subsection (2).)

† The general effect of these enactments is stated at p. 99 of the Introduction.

‡ S. 247 of the Public Health Act, 1875, requires notice of the audit to be given by advertisement in a newspaper. It also requires the auditor to make a report on the accounts to the authority on whose behalf they are submitted, and the clerk to publish an abstract of the accounts in a newspaper. In the case of a parish meeting or council, the expense of the advertisements seems unnecessary; but the enactment in the text will enable the Local Government Board to modify the requirements of the section.

(4.) Every parochial elector of a rural parish may, at all reasonable times, without payment, inspect and take copies of and extracts from all books, accounts, and documents belonging to or under the control of the parish council of the parish or parish meeting.

(5.) Every parochial elector of a parish in a rural district may, at all reasonable times, without payment, inspect and take copies of and extracts from all books, accounts, and documents belonging to or under the control of the district council of the district.

59.—*Supplemental provisions as to district councils.*—(1.) Section one hundred and ninety-nine and Schedule I. of the Public Health Act, 1875, so far as that schedule is unrepealed* (which relate to the meetings of urban authorities, and to the meetings and proceedings of local boards), shall apply in the case of every urban district council other than a borough council and of every rural district council and board of guardians, as if such district council or board were a local board, except that the chairman of the council or board may be elected from outside the councillors or guardians.

(2.) Any urban district council other than a borough council, and any rural district council and board of guardians may, if they think fit, appoint a vice-chairman, to hold office during the term of office of the chairman,† and the vice-chairman shall, in the absence or during the inability of

---

* The Schedule is repealed so far as it relates to committees, by the present Act.

† The chairman will be elected for one year at the annual meeting (38 & 39 Vict. c. 55, Sched. I, Part I (3).)

the chairman, have the powers and authority of the chairman.

(3.) Any rural district council shall be entitled to use for the purpose of their meetings and proceedings the board room and offices of any board of guardians for the union comprising their district at all reasonable hours, and if any question arises as to what hours are reasonable it may be determined by the Local Government Board.

(4.) Nothing in this section shall affect any powers of the Local Government Board with respect to the proceedings of guardians.

(5.) If any district council, other than a borough council, become unable to act, whether from failure to elect or otherwise, the county council of the county in which the district is situate may order elections to be held and may appoint persons to form the district council until the newly elected members come into office.

(6.) Nothing in this Act shall affect any powers of the Secretary of State under the Public Health Supplemental Act for Aldershot, 1857, or the position of persons nominated under those powers.*

Miscellaneous.

60.—*Supplemental provisions as to guardians.*— (1.) The council of each county may, from time to time, by order, fix or alter the number of guardians or rural district councillors to be elected for each parish within their county, and for those purposes may exercise powers of adding parishes

---

* The Aldershot Local Board includes members nominated by the Secretary of State for War.

to each other and dividing parishes into wards, similar to those which by the Acts relating to the relief of the poor are, for the purpose of the election of guardians, vested in the Local Government Board.*

(2.) The council of each county may for the purpose of regulating the retirement of guardians or rural district councillors, in cases where they retire by thirds, and in order that as nearly as may be one-third of the persons elected as guardians for the union, and one-third of the persons elected as rural district councillors for the district, shall retire in each year, direct in which year or years of each triennial period the guardians or district councillors for each parish, ward, or other area in the union or rural district shall retire.

(3.) Where a poor law union is situate in more than one county, the power under this section of fixing or altering the number of guardians or rural district councillors, and of regulating the retirement of guardians and of district councillors, shall be exercised by a joint committee of the councils of the counties concerned, but if any of those councils do not, within two months after request from any other of them, appoint members of such joint committee, the members of the committee actually appointed shall act as the joint committee.

* Parishes of not more than 300 inhabitants may be added to adjoining parishes in the same union for the election of guardians (31 & 32 Vict. c. 122, s. 6). It will be observed that the county council cannot properly, under this provision, add a rural parish to an urban parish, or *vice versâ*. Any parish may be divided into wards for the election of guardians under 39 & 40 Vict. c. 61, s. 12.

Provided that if any order under this subsection is, within six weeks after the making thereof, objected to by any of the county councils concerned, or by any committee of any of those councils authorised in that behalf, it shall be of no effect until confirmed by the Local Government Board.

(4.) Where under any local and personal Act guardians of a poor law union are elected for districts, whether called by that name or not, the provisions of this Act with respect to the election of guardians shall apply as if each of the districts were a parish.

(5.) The board of guardians of a union elected in pursuance of this Act shall, save as otherwise provided by an order of the Local Government Board, made on the application of those guardians, have the same powers and duties under any local and personal Act as the existing board of guardians.

(6.) Nothing in this Act shall alter the constitution of the corporation of the guardians of the poor within the city of Oxford, or the election or qualification of the members thereof, except those members who are elected by the ratepayers of parishes.*

61.—*Place of meeting of parish or district council or board of guardians.*—No parish meeting or meeting of a parish council, or of a district council, or of a board of guardians shall be held in premises licensed for the sale of intoxicating liquor, except in cases where no other suitable room is available

---

* The Oxford Poor Law Incorporation includes representatives of the town council and university.

for such meeting either free of charge or at a reasonable cost.

62.—*Permissive transfer to urban district council of powers of other authorities.*—(1.) Where there is in any urban district, or part of an urban district, any authority constituted under any of the adoptive Acts,* the council of that district may resolve that the powers, duties, property, debts, and liabilities of that authority shall be transferred to the council as from the date specified in the resolution, and upon that date the same shall be transferred accordingly, and the authority shall cease to exist, and the council shall be the successors of that authority.

(2.) After the appointed day any of the adoptive Acts shall not be adopted for any part of an urban district without the approval of the council of that district.

63.—*Provisions as to county council acquiring powers of district council.*—(1.) Where the powers of a district council are by virtue of a resolution under this Act transferred to a county council,† the following provisions shall have effect:—

(a) Notice of the resolution of the county council by virtue of which the transfer is made shall be forthwith sent to the district council and to the Local Government Board:

(b) The expenses incurred by the county council shall be a debt from the district council

---

* *e.g* a burial board. The Adoptive Acts are defined by s. 7.

† *See* ss. 16, 26.

to the county council, and shall be defrayed as part of the expenses of the district council in the execution of the Public Health Acts, and the district council shall have the like power of raising the money as for the defraying of those expenses :

(*c*) The county council for the purpose of the powers transferred may on behalf of the district council borrow subject to the like conditions, in the like manner, and on the security of the like fund or rate, as the district council might have borrowed for the purpose of those powers :

(*d*) The county council may charge the said fund or rate with the payment of the principal and interest of the loan, and the loan with the interest thereon shall be paid by the district council in like manner, and the charge shall have the like effect, as if the loan were lawfully raised and charged on that fund or rate by the district council :

(*e*) The county council shall keep separate accounts of all receipts and expenditure in respect of the said powers :

(*f*) The county council may by order vest in the district council all or any of the powers, duties, property, debts, and liabilities of the county council in relation to any of the said powers, and the property, debts, and liabilities so vested shall be deemed to have been acquired or incurred by the district council for the purpose of those powers.

(2.) Where a rural district is situate in two or

more counties a parish council complaining under this Act may complain to the county council of the county in which the parish is situate, and if the subject-matter of the complaint affects any other county the complaint shall be referred to a joint committee of the councils of the counties concerned, and any question arising as to the constitution of such joint committee shall be determined by the Local Government Board, and if any members of the joint committee are not appointed the members who are actually appointed shall act as the joint committee.

64.—*Power to act through district council.*—A county council may employ a district council as their agents in the transaction of any administrative business on matters arising in, or affecting the interests of, its own district.*

65.—*Saving for harbour powers.*—Where any improvement commission affected by this Act have any powers, duties, property, debts, or liabilities in respect of any harbour, the improvement commission shall continue to exist and be elected for the purpose thereof, and shall continue as a separate body, as if this Act had not passed, and the property, debts, and liabilities shall be apportioned between the district council for the district and the commission so continuing, and the adjustment arising out of the apportionment shall be determined in manner provided by this Act.†

66.—*Saving for elementary schools.*—Nothing in

* *Cf.* s. 28 of the Act of 1888, under which the county council have power to " delegate " powers to the district council.
† *See* s. 68.

this Act shall affect the trusteeship, management, or control of any elementary school.*

67.—*Transfer of property and debts and liabilities.*—Where any powers and duties are transferred by this Act from one authority to another authority—

> (1.) All property held by the first authority for the purpose or by virtue of such powers and duties shall pass to and vest in the other authority, subject to all debts and liabilities affecting the same; and
>
> (2.) The latter authority shall hold the same for the estate, interest, and purposes, and subject to the covenants, conditions, and restrictions for and subject to which the property would have been held if this Act had not passed, so far as the same are not modified by or in pursuance of this Act; and
>
> (3.) All debts and liabilities of the first authority incurred by virtue of such powers and duties shall become debts and liabilities of the latter authority, and be defrayed out of the like property and funds out of which they would have been defrayed if this Act had not passed.

68.—*Adjustment of property and liabilities.*—(1.) Where any adjustment is required for the purpose

---

* *i.e.* a school at which elementary education is the principal part of the education there given, and where the ordinary payments in respect of the instruction, from each scholar, do not exceed 9d. a week (Elementary Education Act, 1870, s. 3 and s. 75 of the present Act).

of this Act, or of any order, or thing made or done under this Act, then, if the adjustment is not otherwise made, the authorities interested may make agreements for the purpose, and may thereby adjust any property, income, debts, liabilities, and expenses, so far as affected by this Act, or such scheme, order, or thing, of the parties to the agreement.

(2.) The agreement may provide for the transfer or retention of any property, debts, or liabilities, with or without any conditions, and for the joint use of any property, and for payment by either party to the agreement in respect of property, debts, and liabilities so transferred or retained, or of such joint user, and in respect of the salary or remuneration of any officer or person, and that either by way of an annual payment or, except in the case of a salary or remuneration, by way of a capital sum, or of a terminable annuity for a period not exceeding that allowed by the Local Government Board: Provided that where any of the authorities interested is a board of guardians, any such agreement, so far as it relates to the joint use of any property, shall be subject to the approval of the Local Government Board.

(3.) In default of an agreement, and as far as any such agreement does not extend, such adjustment shall be referred to arbitration in accordance with the Arbitration Act, 1889,* and the arbitrator shall have power to disallow as costs in the arbitration the costs of any witness whom he considers to have been called unnecessarily, and any other costs which he considers to have been incurred unnecessarily, and his award may provide

---

* 52 & 53 Vict. c. 49.

for any matter for which an agreement might have provided.

(4.) Any sum required to be paid by any authority for the purpose of adjustment may be paid as part of the general expenses of exercising their duties under this Act, or out of such special fund as the authority, with the approval of the Local Government Board, direct, and if it is a capital sum the payment thereof shall be a purpose for which the authority may borrow under the Acts relating to such authority, on the security of all or any of the funds, rates, and revenues of the authority, and any such sum may be borrowed without the consent of any authority, so that it be repaid within such period as the Local Government Board may sanction.

(5.) Any capital sum paid to any authority for the purpose of any adjustment under this Act shall be treated as capital, and applied, with the sanction of the Local Government Board, either in the repayment of debt or for any other purpose for which capital money may be applied.

69.—*Power to deal with matters arising out of alteration of boundaries.*—Where an alteration of any area is made by this Act, an order for any of the matters mentioned in section fifty-nine of the Local Government Act, 1888,* may, if it appears to the county council desirable, be made by the county council, or, in the case of an area situate in more than one county, by a joint committee of county councils, but nothing in this section shall empower a county council or joint committee to alter the boundaries of a county.

* *See* this section n the Appendix,

70.—*Summary proceeding for determination of questions as to transfer of powers.*—(1.) If any question arises, or is about to arise, as to whether any power, duty, or liability is or is not transferred by or under this Act to any parish council, parish meeting, or district council, or any property is or is not vested in the parish council, or in the chairman and overseers of a rural parish, or in a district council, that question, without prejudice to any other mode of trying it, may, on the application of the council, meeting, or other local authority concerned, be submitted for decision to the High Court in such summary manner as, subject to any rules of court, may be directed by the Court; and the Court, after hearing such parties and taking such evidence (if any) as it thinks just, shall decide the question.*

(2.) If any question arises or is about to arise under this Act as to the appointment of the trustees or beneficiaries of any charity, or as to the persons in whom the property of any charity is vested, such question shall, at the request of any trustee, beneficiary, or other person interested, be determined in the first instance by the Charity Commissioners, subject to an appeal to the High Court brought within three months after such determination. Provided that an appeal to the High Court of Justice from any determination of the Charity Commissioners under this section may

---

* Under a similar provision in s. 29 of the Local Government Act, 1888, the Court has decided numerous questions submitted to it with regard to the transfer of powers under that Act. The present Act—differing in this respect from the Act of 1888 (*see Ex parte* the county council of Kent and the councils of Dover and Sandwich [1891], 1 Q. B. 725)—gives an appeal against the decision of the High Court in such cases.

be presented only under the same conditions as are prescribed in the case of appeals to the High Court from orders made by the Charity Commissioners under the Charitable Trusts Acts, 1853 to 1891.*

(3.) An appeal shall, with the leave of the High Court or Court of Appeal, but not otherwise, lie to the Court of Appeal against any decision under this section.

71.—*Supplemental provisions as to county council orders.*—A copy of every order made by a county council or joint committee in pursuance of this Act shall be sent to the Local Government Board, and, if it alters any local area or name, also to the Board of Agriculture.†

72.—*Provisions as to local inquiries.*—(1.) The expenses incurred by the Local Government Board in respect of inquiries or other proceedings under this Act shall be paid by such authorities and persons and out of such funds and rates as the Board may by order direct, and the Board may certify the amount of the expenses so incurred, and any sum so certified and directed by the Board to be paid by any authority or person shall be a debt from that authority or person to the Crown.‡

(2.) Such expenses may include the salary of

---

* Twenty-one days' notice of the intention to appeal must be given to the Commissioners and to the solicitor acting for the Attorney-General in *ex-officio* proceedings relating to charities (23 & 24 Vict. c. 136, s. 8; 32 & 33 Vict. c. 110, s. 11).

† Orders will be made by joint committees under ss. 20, 36, and 60.

‡ Similar provisions are contained in s. 87 of the Act of 1888.

any inspector or officer of the Board engaged in the inquiry or proceeding, not exceeding three guineas a day.*

(3.) The Local Government Board and their inspectors shall have for the purposes of an inquiry in pursuance of this Act the same powers as they respectively have for the purpose of an inquiry under the Public Health Act, 1875.*

(4.) Where a county council hold a local inquiry under this Act or under the Local Government Act, 1888, on the application of the council of a parish or district, or of any inhabitants of a parish or district, the expenses incurred by the county council in relation to the inquiry (including the expenses of any committee or person authorised by the county council) shall be paid by the council of that parish or district, or, in the case of a parish which has not a parish council, by the parish meeting; but, save as aforesaid, the expenses of the county council incurred in the case of inquiries under this Act shall be paid out of the county fund.†

73.—*Provision as to Sundays and bank holidays.*—When the day on which anything is required by or in pursuance of this Act to be done is Sunday, Christmas Day, or Good Friday, or a bank holiday, that thing shall be done on the next following day, not being one of the days above mentioned.

74.—*Provisions as to Scilly Islands.*—This Act

* *See* note (‡) on previous page.

† The Act of 1888 does not provide for the expenses incurred by county councils in connection with inquiries under that Act, although s. 87 provides for expenses of the Local Government Board. This omission is now remedied.

shall be deemed to be an Act touching local government within the meaning of section forty-nine of the Local Government Act, 1888, and a provisional order for the Scilly Islands may, on the application of the council of the Isles of Scilly, and after such public notice as appears to the Local Government Board sufficient for giving information to all persons interested, be made accordingly.*

75.—*Construction of Act.*—(1.) The definition of " parish " in section one hundred of the Local Government Act, 1888, shall not apply to this Act,† but, save as aforesaid, expressions used in this Act shall, unless the context otherwise requires, have the same meaning as in the said Act.

(2.) In this Act, unless the context otherwise requires—

> Any reference to population means the population according to the census of one thousand eight hundred and ninety-one.
> The expression " parochial elector," when used with reference to a parish in an urban district, or in the county of London or any county borough, means any person who would be a parochial elector of the parish if it were a rural parish.
> The expression " election " includes both the nomination and the poll.
> The expression " trustees " includes persons

---

* *i.e.*, this Act may be applied to the Scilly Islands by a provisional order of the Local Government Board.

† By section 5 of the Interpretation Act, 1889, " parish " is defined to mean a place for which a separate poor rate is or can be made, or for which a separate overseer is or can be appointed.

administering or managing any charity or recreation ground, or other property or thing in relation to which the word is used.

The expression "ecclesiastical charity" includes a charity, the endowment whereof is held for some one or more of the following purposes:—

(*a*) for any spiritual purpose which is a legal purpose; or

(*b*) for the benefit of any spiritual person or ecclesiastical officer as such; or

(*c*) for use, if a building, as a church, chapel, mission room, or Sunday school, or otherwise by any particular church or denomination; or

(*d*) for the maintenance, repair, or improvement of any such building as aforesaid, or for the maintenance of divine service therein; or

(*e*) otherwise for the benefit of any particular church or denomination, or of any members thereof as such.

Provided that where any endowment of a charity other than a building held for any of the purposes aforesaid, is held in part only for some of the purposes aforesaid, the charity, so far as that endowment is concerned, shall be an ecclesiastical charity within the meaning of this Act; and the Charity Commissioners shall, on application by any person interested, make such provision for the apportionment and management of that endowment as seems to them necessary or expedient for giving effect to this Act.

The expression shall also include any building

which in the opinion of the Charity Commissioners has been erected or provided within forty years before the passing of this Act mainly by or at the cost of members of any particular church or denomination.

The expression "affairs of the church" shall include the distribution of offertories or other collections made in any church.

The expression "parochial charity" means a charity the benefits of which are or the separate distribution of the benefits of which is confined to inhabitants of a single parish, or of a single ancient ecclesiastical parish divided into two or more parishes, or of not more than five neighbouring parishes.*

The expression "vestry" in relation to a parish means the inhabitants of the parish whether in vestry assembled or not, and includes any select vestry either by statute or at common law.

The expression "rateable value" means the rateable value stated in the valuation list in force, or, if there is no such list, in the last poor rate.

The expression "county" includes a county borough, and the expression "county council" includes the council of a county borough.

* Probably a narrower definition would have excluded some existing charities that may not improperly be termed "parochial," and it is believed that the definition was not settled until the actual circumstances of particular charities had been considered.

The expression "elementary school" means an elementary school within the meaning of the Elementary Education Act, 1870.*

The expression "local and personal Act" includes a Provisional Order confirmed by an Act and the Act confirming the Order.

The expression "prescribed" means prescribed by order of the Local Government Board.

76.—*Extent of Act.*—This Act shall not extend to Scotland or Ireland.

77.—*Short title.*—This Act may be cited as the Local Government Act, 1894.

PART V.

Transitory Provisions.

78.—*First elections to parish councils.*—(1.) The overseers of each rural parish shall convene the first parish meeting of the parish at the time fixed by or under this Act for the first election of parish councillors, whether there is or is not a parish council for the parish, and for this purpose the overseers of a parish shall be deemed to be the overseers of every part of the parish.†

(2.) The chairman of the parish meeting at which the first parish councillors are nominated, or in his default the clerk of the guardians, shall convene the first meeting of the parish council.

---

* *See* note to s. 66.

† This provides for parishes divided by s. 1 (3).

(3.) The first parish councillors and the first chairman of a parish meeting elected under this Act shall retire on the second ordinary day of coming into office of councillors* which happens after their election.

79.—*First elections of guardians and district councils.*—(1.) The existing boards of guardians and urban and rural sanitary authorities shall take the necessary measures for the conduct of the first elections of guardians and district councillors respectively under this Act, including any appointment of returning officers required by rules under this Act.†

(2.) Where a parish is divided by this Act into two or more new parishes, then, subject to any order made by the county council, there shall be one guardian, and if it is in a rural district, one district councillor for each of such new parishes.‡

(3.) Of the guardians and urban and rural district councillors first elected under this Act, save as hereinafter mentioned, one-third as nearly as may be shall continue in office until the fifteenth day of April one thousand eight hundred and ninety-six, and shall then retire; and one-third as nearly as may be shall continue in office until the fifteenth day of April one thousand eight hundred and ninety-seven, and shall then retire, and the remainder shall continue in office until the fifteenth day of April one thousand eight hundred and ninety-eight, and shall then retire.

(4). The guardians and rural district councillors

---

* *i.e.* 15th April, 1896. (*See* s. 3 (4).)
† *See* s. 48.
‡ This applies to parishes divided by ss. 1 (3), 36 (2).

to retire respectively on the fifteenth day of April one thousand eight hundred and ninety-six and on the fifteenth day of April one thousand eight hundred and ninety-seven shall be the guardians and rural district councillors for such parishes, wards, or other areas, as may be determined by the county council for the purpose of the rotation.

(5.) Where guardians or rural district councillors retire together at the end of the triennial period, the guardians and district councillors first elected under this Act shall retire on the fifteenth day of April one thousand eight hundred and ninety-eight.

(6.) Of the first urban district councillors elected under this Act, the third who are respectively to retire on the fifteenth day of April one thousand eight hundred and ninety-six and one thousand eight hundred and ninety-seven shall be determined according to their place on the poll at the election, those that were lowest on the poll retiring first. If there was no poll, or if a question arises in consequence of an equality of votes between two or more councillors, the matter shall be determined by ballot conducted under the direction of the council.

(7.) In the case of an urban district divided into wards, the foregoing provisions with respect to retirement shall apply separately to each ward.

(8.) Upon the day on which the first guardians and urban or rural district councillors elected under this Act come into office,* the persons who are then members of boards of guardians, and urban and rural sanitary authorities, shall cease to hold office,

* *See* page 102 of the Introduction.

but until that day the persons who are at the passing of this Act guardians and members of urban sanitary authorities (for urban districts not being boroughs) and of highway boards shall continue in office notwithstanding any want of qualification, as if the term of office for which they were elected expired on that day, and, except for the purpose of filling casual vacancies or electing additional guardians, no further elections shall be held.*

(9.) The first meeting of each district council elected under this Act shall be convened by the returning officer.

(10.) The foregoing provisions shall apply to the existing members and first members elected under this Act of the local board of Woolwich and of any vestry under the Metropolis Management Acts, 1855 to 1890, and any Act amending the same, and to the existing and first auditors elected under those Acts in like manner as if they were members of urban sanitary authorities or urban district councillors, as the case may require, except that the date of the annual election shall be substituted for the fifteenth day of April.

* Circulars have been issued by the Local Government Board to boards of guardians, urban sanitary authorities (other than town councils), highway boards, metropolitan vestries and district boards, &c , explaining the effect of this subsection. We have mentioned (see note to s. 50) that the appointment of overseers by the justices was to take place this year as usual. It should also be noticed that in separate highway parishes a surveyor or surveyors of highways should have been elected at the usual time this year. Members of burial boards and inspectors under the Lighting and Watching Act must likewise, until November next, be appointed at the usual time, notwithstanding anything in the Act,

(11.) The overseers of any parish divided by this Act shall, until the first appointment of overseers next after the appointed day, continue in office as if they were overseers of each part of the said parish, which by reason of such division becomes a separate parish.*

80.—*Power of county council to remove difficulties.*—(1.) If any difficulty arises with respect to the holding of the first parish meeting of a rural parish, or to the first election of parish or district councillors, or of guardians, or of members of the local board of Woolwich, or any vestry in the county of London, or of auditors in the county of London, or to the first meeting of a parish or district council, or board of guardians, or such local board or vestry as aforesaid, or if, from no election being held or an election being defective or otherwise, the first parish or district council, or board of guardians, or local board or vestry has not been properly constituted, or there are no auditors under the Metropolis Management Acts, 1855 to 1890, or an insufficient number, properly elected, the county council may by order make any appointment or do any thing which appears to them necessary or expedient for the proper holding of any such first meeting or election and properly constituting the parish or district council, board of guardians, local board, or vestry, or auditors, and may, if it appears to them necessary, direct the holding of a meeting or election, and fix the dates for any such meeting or election, but a parish shall, notwithstanding any such failure to constitute the parish council,

* *See* note to subsection (2). Separate overseers for the new parishes formed by the division will not be appointed until the usual time in 1895. The note to s. 50 may be referred to,

be deemed to be a parish having a parish council within the meaning of this Act. Any such order may modify the provisions of this Act, and the enactments applied by or rules framed under this Act so far as may appear to the county council necessary or expedient for carrying the order into effect.

(2.) The Local Government Board shall make regulations for expediting and simplifying the procedure under section fifty-seven of the Local Government Act, 1888, in all cases in the year one thousand eight hundred and ninety-four, for the purpose of bringing this Act into immediate operation, and such regulations may dispense with the final approval of an order by the county council in cases where the prescribed notice of the proposed order has been given before it is made by the county council.

81.—*Existing officers.*—(1.) Where the powers and duties of any authority other than justices are transferred by this Act to any parish or district council, the officers of that authority shall become the officers of that council, and for the purposes of this section the body appointing a surveyor of highways shall be deemed to be a highway authority and any paid surveyor to be an officer of that body.*

(2.) Where there is in a rural parish an existing vestry clerk appointed under the Vestries Act, 1850, he shall become the clerk of the parish council, and if there is also an assistant overseer in the parish, then, notwithstanding the foregoing

* A surveyor of parish highways appointed under s. 9 of the Highway Act, 1835 (5 & 6 Will. IV, c. 50), appears to be within this clause.

provisions of this Act,* that assistant overseer shall not, while such vestry clerk holds office, be the clerk of the parish council.

(3.) Any existing assistant overseer in a parish for which a parish council is elected shall, unless appointed by a board of guardians, become an officer of the parish council.

(4.) Every such officer, vestry clerk, and assistant overseer, as above in this section mentioned shall hold his office by the same tenure and upon the same terms and conditions as heretofore, and while performing the same duties shall receive not less salary or remuneration than heretofore.

(5.) Where a parish or rural sanitary district is divided by this Act,† any officer for the parish or district so divided shall hold his office as such officer for each parish or district formed by the division, and his salary shall be borne by the respective parishes or districts in proportion to their rateable value at the commencement of the local financial year next after the passing of this Act.

(6.) So much of any enactment as authorises the appointment of assistant overseers by a board of guardians shall be repealed as from the appointed day.‡

(7.) Section one hundred and twenty of the Local Government Act, 1888,§ which relates to compensation to existing officers, shall apply in the case of existing officers affected by this Act,

---

* The provisions referred to are those of s. 17.

† *i.e.* under ss. 1 (3), 24 (5), or 36 (2).

‡ This will not affect present office-holders (Interpretation Act, 1889, s. 38).

§ *See* this section in the Appendix.

whether officers above in this section mentioned or not, as if references in that section to the county council were references to the parish council, or the district council, or board of guardians or other authority whose officer the person affected is when the claim for compensation arises as the case may require. Provided that all expenses incurred by a district council in pursuance of this section shall be paid as general expenses of the council, and any expenses incurred by a board of guardians in pursuance of this section shall be paid out of their common fund, and any expenses incurred by any other authority in pursuance of this section shall be paid out of the fund applicable to payment of the salary of the offices affected.

82.—*Provision as to highways.*—(1.) Where before the appointed day the highway expenses were charged on a particular parish or other area and not on a district, the district council may determine that the highways in that parish or area shall be placed in proper repair before the expenses of repairing the same become a charge upon the district, and, failing such highways being placed in proper repair to the satisfaction of the district council, the district council may themselves place the highways in proper repair, and the expense incurred by them of placing those highways in proper repair shall be a separate charge on the parish or area, and any question which arises as to whether any such expenses are properly a separate charge on the parish or area shall be determined by the county council.

(2.) Where in pursuance of an order of a county council a parish continues to maintain its own highways after the appointed day, the highway expenses shall not be deemed to be expenses of the parish council or of the parish meeting within the meaning of this Act.*

83.—*Duty of county council to bring Act into operation.*—It shall be the duty of every county council to exercise all such of their powers as may be requisite for bringing this Act into full operation within their county as soon as may be after the passing thereof, and a county council may delegate their powers under this Act to a committee.

84.—*Appointed day.*—(1.) The first elections under this Act shall be held on the eighth day of November next after the passing of this Act, or such later date or dates in the year one thousand eight hundred and ninety-four as the Local Government Board may fix.†

(2.) The persons elected shall come into office on the second Thursday next after their election, or such other day not more than seven days earlier or later as may be fixed by or in pursuance of the rules made under this Act in relation to their election.‡

(3.) Every division into wards or alteration of the boundaries of any parish or union or district which is to affect the first election shall, if it affects the parishes or parts for which the registers of parochial electors will be made, be made so far as practicable before the first day of July next after the passing of this Act, and any such

---

* A parish not within a highway district will continue to maintain its highways where an order is made under s. 25, postponing the operation of that section as to highway matters. The reference in the last three lines is to ss. 11 and 19.

† The remarks at page 102 of the Introduction should be referred to.   ‡ *i.e.* rules made under s. 48.

division or alteration which after the appointed day may be made on application by the parish council or any parochial electors of any parish, may be made before the appointed day on application by the vestry or a like number of the ratepayers of the parish.*

Provided that—

    (a) If any county council having any such division or alteration under consideration so direct, the lists of voters shall be framed in parts corresponding with such division or alteration so that the parts may serve either for the unaltered parish, union, or district, or for the same when divided or altered ; and

    (b) If the county council making such division or alteration on or after the said day and on or before the last day of August one thousand eight hundred and ninety-four so direct, the clerk of the county council shall make such adjustment of the registers of parochial electors as the division or alteration may render necessary for enabling every parochial elector to vote at the first election in the ward, union, or district in which his qualification is situate, and in that case the said division or alteration shall be observed in the case of that election.

(4.) Subject as in this Act mentioned, " the appointed day " shall,

* It is to be regretted that a similar provision has not been made for applications before the appointed day for grouping orders and orders for the establishment of parish councils in parishes of less than 300 inhabitants.

(a) for the purpose of elections and of parish meetings in parishes not having a parish council, be the day or respective days fixed for the first elections under this Act, or such prior day as may be necessary for the purpose of giving notices or doing other acts preliminary to such elections; and

(b) for the purpose of the powers, duties, and liabilities of councils or other bodies elected under this Act, or other matters not specifically mentioned, be the day on which the members of such councils or other bodies first elected under this Act come into office; and

(c) for the purpose of powers, duties, and liabilities transferred to a council of a borough by this Act, be the first day of November next after the passing of this Act;

and the lists and registers of parochial electors shall be made out in such parts as may be necessary for the purpose of the first elections under this Act.

Provided that where an order of a county council postpones the operation of the section with respect to highways as respects their county or any part thereof* the day on which such postponement ceases shall, as respects such county or part, be the appointed day, and the order of postponement shall make such provision as may be necessary for holding elections of highway boards during the interval before the appointed day.†

* An order under s. 25 (1) is referred to.

† This will enable the county council to give directions for

85.—*Current rates, &c.*—(1.) Every rate and precept for contributions made before the appointed day may be assessed, levied, and collected, and proceedings for the enforcement thereof taken, in like manner as nearly as may be as if this Act had not passed.

(2.) The accounts of all receipts and expenditure before the appointed day shall be audited, and disallowances, surcharges,* and penalties recovered and enforced, and other consequential proceedings had, in like manner as nearly as may be as if this Act had not passed, but as soon as practicable after the appointed day; and every authority, committee, or officer whose duty it is to make up any accounts, or to account for any portion of the receipts or expenditure in any account, shall, until the audit is completed, be deemed for the purpose of such audit to continue in office, and be bound to perform the same duties and render the same accounts and be subject to the same liabilities as before the appointed day.

(3.) All proceedings, legal and other, commenced before the appointed day, may be carried on in like manner, as nearly as may be, as if this Act had not passed, and any such legal proceeding may be amended in such manner as may appear necessary or proper in order to bring it into conformity with the provisions of this Act.

---

the election of waywardens in place of those who will cease to hold office when the rural district councillors come into office, and also to order for what period such waywardens shall be elected, having regard to the period of postponement.—*Circular of Local Government Board, 9th March, 1894.*

* As to disallowances and surcharges, *see* the remarks on p. 99 of the Introduction.

(4.) Every valuation list made for a parish divided by this Act shall continue in force until a new valuation list is made.

(5.) The change of name of an urban sanitary authority shall not affect their identity as a corporate body or derogate from their powers, and any enactment in any Act, whether public general or local and personal, referring to the members of such authority shall, unless inconsistent with this Act, continue to refer to the members of such authority under its new name.

86.—*Saving for existing securities and discharge of debts.*—(1.) Nothing in this Act shall prejudicially affect any securities granted before the passing of this Act on the credit of any rate or property transferred to a council or parish meeting by this Act; and all such securities, as well as all unsecured debts, liabilities, and obligations incurred by any authority in the exercise of any powers or in relation to any property transferred from them to a council or parish meeting shall be discharged, paid, and satisfied by that council or parish meeting, and where for that purpose it is necessary to continue the levy of any rate or the exercise of any power which would have existed but for this Act, that rate may continue to be levied and that power to be exercised either by the authority who otherwise would have levied or exercised the same, or by the transferee as the case may require.

(2.) It shall be the duty of every authority whose powers, duties, and liabilities are transferred by this Act to liquidate so far as practicable before the appointed day, all current debts and liabilities incurred by such authority.

87.—*Saving for existing byelaws.*—All such byelaws, orders, and regulations of any authority, whose powers and duties are transferred by this Act to any council, as are in force at the time of the transfer, shall, so far as they relate to or are in pursuance of the powers and duties transferred, continue in force as if made by that council, and may be revoked or altered accordingly.

88.—*Saving for pending contracts, &c.*—(1.) If at the time when any powers, duties, liabilities debts, or property are by this Act transferred to a council or parish meeting, any action or proceeding, or any cause of action or proceeding is pending or existing by or against any authority in relation thereto the same shall not be in anywise prejudicially affected by the passing of this Act, but may be continued, prosecuted, and enforced by or against the council or parish meeting as successors of the said authority in like manner as if this Act had not been passed.

(2.) All contracts, deeds, bonds, agreements, and other instruments subsisting at the time of the transfer in this section mentioned, and affecting any of such powers, duties, liabilities, debts, or property, shall be of as full force and effect against or in favour of the council or parish meeting, and may be enforced as fully and effectually as if, instead of the authority, the council or parish meeting had been a party thereto.

89.—*Repeal.*—The Acts specified in the Second Schedule to this Act are hereby repealed as from the appointed day to the extent in the third column of that schedule mentioned, and so much of any Act, whether public general or local and personal, as is inconsistent with this Act is also hereby repealed. Provided that where any wards of an urban district have been created, or any number of members of an urban sanitary authority fixed, by or in pursuance of any local and personal Act, such wards and number of members shall continue and be alterable in like manner as if they had been fixed by an order of the county council under this or any other Act.*

* We have not thought it necessary to print Schedule II in our copy of the Act, as it is long and deals chiefly with enactments superseded by the Act. The most important repeals are referred to in the Introduction.

SCHEDULES.

FIRST SCHEDULE.

Rules as to Parish Meetings, Parish Councils, and Committees.

Part One.

*Rules applicable to Parish Meetings.**

(1.) The annual assembly of the parish meeting shall be held on the twenty-fifth day of March in each year, or within seven days before or after that day.

(2.) Not less than seven clear days before any parish meeting, public notice thereof shall be given specifying the time and place of the intended meeting and the business to be transacted at the meeting, and signed by the chairman of the parish council or other conveners of the meeting.

(3.) If the business relates to the establishment or dissolution of a parish council, or the grouping of a parish, or the adoption of any of the adoptive Acts, not less than fourteen days' notice shall be given.

(4.) A parish meeting may discuss parish affairs and pass resolutions thereon.

(5.) Every question to be decided by a parish meeting shall, in the first instance, be decided by the majority of those present and voting on the question, and the chairman shall announce his decision as to the result, and that decision shall be final, unless a poll is demanded.

(6.) A poll may be demanded at any time before the conclusion of a parish meeting.

* *See* s. 2 (7).

(7.) A poll may be demanded by any one parochial elector in the case of a resolution respecting any of the following matters, namely:—

- (a) Any application, representation, or complaint to a county council or district council;*
- (b) The appointment of a chairman for the year or of a committee, or the delegation of any powers or duties to a committee, or the approval of the acts of a committee;
- (c) The appointment of an overseer, the appointment or revocation of the appointment or dismissal of an assistant overseer or a parish officer;
- (d) The appointment of trustees or beneficiaries of a charity;
- (e) The adoption of any of the adoptive Acts;
- (f) The formation or dissolution of a school board;
- (g) The consent or refusal of consent to any act, matter, or thing which cannot by law be done without that consent;†
- (h) The incurring of any expense or liability;
- (i) The place and time for the assembly of the parish meeting;
- (k) Any other prescribed matter; ‡

but, save as aforesaid, a poll shall not be taken unless either the chairman of the meeting assents, or the poll is demanded by parochial electors present at the meeting, not being less than five in number or one-third of those present, whichever number is least.

(8.) In case of an equal division of votes at a parish meeting, the chairman shall have a second or casting vote.

(9.) Where a parish meeting is held for the election of parish councillors, opportunity shall be given at the meeting for putting questions to such of the candidates as are present,

---

* *e.g.*, an application for the powers of a parish council (s. 19), or for a grouping order, or an order creating a parish council (s. 38); a representation as to the stopping of a right of way (ss. 19, 26); a complaint of default on the part of a district council to perform their duties (ss. 16, 19).

† *e.g.*, consent to the making of a grouping order or an order creating a parish council, or to the incurring by the parish council (if any) of any expense or liability (ss. 1, 11).

‡ *i.e.* prescribed by the Local Government Board (s. 75).

and receiving explanations from them, and any candidate shall be entitled to attend the meeting and speak thereat, but, unless he is a parochial elector, not to vote.

(10.) If the chairman of the parish meeting is absent from or unwilling or unable to take the chair at any assembly of the parish meeting, the meeting may appoint a person to take the chair, and that person shall have, for the purpose of that meeting, the powers and authority of the chairman.

(11.) Any notice required to be given to or served on a parish meeting may be given to or served on the chairman of the parish meeting.

PART TWO.

*Rules applicable to Parish Councils.**

(1.) Every parish councillor shall, at the first meeting after his election, or if the council at the first meeting so permit, then at a later meeting fixed by the council, sign, in the presence of some member of the council, a declaration that he accepts the office, and if he does not sign such a declaration his office shall be void.

(2.) If any casual vacancy arises in the council, the council shall forthwith be convened for filling the vacancy.

(3.) The first business at the annual meeting shall be to elect a chairman and to appoint the overseers.

(4.) The chairman may at any time convene a meeting of the parish council If the chairman refuses to convene a meeting of the council after a requisition for that purpose signed by two members of the council has been presented to him, any two members of the council may forthwith, on that refusal, convene a meeting. If the chairman (without so refusing) does not within seven days after such presentation, convene a meeting, any two members of the council may, on the expiration of those seven days, convene a meeting.

(5) Three clear days at least before any meeting of a parish council notice thereof, specifying the time and place of the intended meeting and the business to be transacted at the meeting, and signed by or on behalf of the chairman of the parish council or persons convening the meeting, shall be given to every member of the parish council, and in case of the annual meeting notice specifying the like particulars

* *See* s. 3 (10).

shall be given to every member of the parish council immediately after his election.

(6.) Any notice required by law to be given to the chairman or any other member of the parish council may be left at or sent by post to the usual place of abode of such chairman or member.

(7.) No business shall be transacted at any meeting of a parish council unless at least one-third of the full number of members are present thereat, subject to this qualification, that in no case shall the quorum be less than three.

(8.) The names of the members present at any meeting of the parish council, as well as of those voting on each question on which a division is taken, shall be recorded, so as to show whether each vote given was for or against the question.

(9) Every question at a meeting of a parish council shall be decided by a majority of votes of the members present and voting on that question

(10.) In case of an equal division of votes the chairman of the meeting shall have a second or casting vote.

(11.) The parish council may, if they think fit, appoint one of their number to be vice-chairman, and the vice-chairman shall, in the absence or during the inability of the chairman, have the powers and authority of the chairman.

(12.) The proceedings of a parish council shall not be invalidated by any vacancy among their members, or by any defect in the election or qualification of any member thereof.

(13.) A parish council shall hold not less than four meetings in each year, of which one shall be the annual meeting, and every such meeting shall be open to the public unless the council otherwise direct.

(14.) Every cheque or other order for payment of money by a parish council shall be signed by two members of the council.

(15.) Any notice required to be given to or served on a parish council may be given to or served on the clerk to the parish council.

(16.) The parish council may appear before any court or in any legal proceeding by their clerk or by any officer or member authorised generally or in respect of any special proceeding by resolution of the council, and their clerk or any member or officer shall, if so authorised, be at liberty to institute and carry on any proceeding which the parish council are authorised to institute and carry on.

Part Three.

General.*

(1.) Minutes of the proceedings of every parish council and parish meeting shall be kept in a book provided for that purpose.

(2.) A minute of proceedings at a meeting of a parish council, or of a committee of a parish or district council, or at a parish meeting, signed at the same or the next ensuing meeting by a person describing himself as or appearing to be chairman of the meeting at which the minute is signed, shall be received in evidence without further proof.

(3.) Until the contrary is proved, every meeting in respect of the proceedings whereof a minute has been so made shall be deemed to have been duly convened and held, and all the members of the meeting shall be deemed to have been duly qualified; and where the proceedings are proceedings of a committee, the committee shall be deemed to have been duly constituted, and to have had power to deal with the matters referred to in the minutes.

(4.) Any instrument purporting to be executed under the hands or under the hands and seals of the chairman and of two other members of a parish council or of a parish meeting shall, until the contrary is proved, be deemed to have been duly so executed.

(5.) Subject to the provisions of this Act, a parish council may make, vary, and revoke standing orders for the regulation of their proceedings and business, and of the proceedings and business at parish meetings for a rural parish having a parish council.

(6.) Where there is no council for a rural parish, the parish meeting may, subject to the provisions of this Act, regulate their own proceedings and business.

Part Four.

Proceedings of Committees of Parish or District Councils.†

(1.) The quorum, proceedings, and place of meeting of a committee, whether within or without the parish or district,

---

* *See* ss. 2 (7), 3 (10). † *See* s. 56 (3).

and the area (if any) within which the committee are to exercise their authority, shall be such as may be determined by regulations of the council or councils appointing the committee.

(2.) Subject to such regulations, the quorum, proceedings, and place of meeting, whether within or without the parish or district, shall be such as the committee direct, and the chairman at any meeting of the committee shall have a second or casting vote.

SECOND SCHEDULE

Enactments Repealed.*

* *See* note to s. 89.

APPENDIX.

LOCAL GOVERNMENT ACT, 1888.

(51 & 52 Vict. c. 41.)

SECTIONS 54, 57, 58, 59, 120.

54.—*Future Alterations of Boundaries.*—(1.) Whenever it is represented by the council of any county or borough to the Local Government Board—

(a) That the alteration of the boundary of any county or borough is desirable; or

* * * * * *

(f) That the alteration of any area of local government partly situate in their county or borough is desirable,

the Local Government Board shall, unless for special reasons they think that the representation ought not to be entertained, cause to be made a local inquiry, and may make an order for the proposal contained in such representation, or for such other proposal as they may deem expedient, or may refuse such order; and if they make the order, may by such order divide or alter any electoral division.*

* * * * * *

* *i.e.* a division for the election of a county councillor.

(3.) Provided that if the order alters the boundary of a county or borough, * * * * * it shall be provisional only, and shall not have effect unless confirmed by Parliament.

(4.) Where such order alters the boundary of a borough it may, as consequential upon such alteration, do all or any of the following things: increase or decrease the number of the wards in the borough, and alter the boundaries of such wards, and alter the apportionment of the number of councillors among the wards, and alter the total number of councillors, and in such case, make the proportionate alteration in the number of aldermen.

57.—*Future Alteration of County Districts and Parishes and Wards, and Future Establishment of Urban Districts.*—(1.) Whenever a county council is satisfied that a *primâ facie* case is made out as respects any county district* not a borough, or as respects any parish, for a proposal for all or any of the following things; that is to say :—

- (*a*) the alteration or definition of the boundary thereof ;
- (*b*) the division thereof or the union thereof with any other such district or districts, parish or parishes, or the transfer of part of a parish to another parish ;
- (*c*) the conversion of any such district or part thereof, if it is a rural district, into an urban district, and if it is an urban district, into a rural district, or the transfer of the whole or any part of any such district from one district to another, and the formation of new urban or rural districts ;
- (*d*) the division of an urban district into wards ; and

---

* *See* the definition of " county district " in s. 21 of the Local Government Act, 1894.

(e) the alteration of the number of wards, or of the boundaries of any ward, or of the number of members of any district council, or of the apportionment of such members among the wards,

the county council may cause such inquiry to be made in the locality, and such notice to be given, both in the locality, and to the Local Government Board, Education Department, or other Government department as may be prescribed,* and such other inquiry and notices (if any) as they think fit, and if satisfied that such proposal is desirable, may make an order for the same accordingly.†

(2.) Notice of the provisions of the order shall be given, and copies thereof shall be supplied in the prescribed manner,* and otherwise as the county council think fit, and if it relates to the division of a district into wards, or the alteration of the number of wards or of the boundaries of a ward, or of the number of the members of a district council, or of the apportionment of the members among the wards,‡ shall come into operation upon being finally approved by the county council.

(3.) In any other case the order shall be submitted

---

* Regulations as to notices under this section were prescribed by order of the Local Government Board in 1889; but section 80 (2) of the new Act requires that Board to make regulations for expediting and simplifying the procedure under s. 57 of the Act of 1888 as regards the present year, and an order for this purpose was issued on the 22nd March, which for the time being takes the place of the order of 1889.

† Section 36 (11) of the Act of 1894 amends this by providing that a joint committee of the county councils may make orders as regards areas in two or more counties, and as regards areas the alteration of which would affect the boundaries of a union in two or more counties. Section 72 (4) of the new Act provides for the expenses of the county council in connection with inquiries.

‡ *i.e.* in the cases provided for in paragraphs (d) and (e) of subsection 1.

to the Local Government Board;* and if within [six weeks]† after such notice of the provisions of the order as the Local Government Board determine to be the first notice, the council of any district affected by the order, or any number of county electors registered in that district or in any ward of that district, not being less than one-sixth of the total number of electors in that district or ward, or if the order relates only to a parish, any number of county electors registered in that parish, not being less than one-sixth of the total number of electors in that parish, petition the Local Government Board to disallow the order,‡ the Local Government Board shall cause to be made a local inquiry, and determine whether the order is to be confirmed or not.

(4.) If any such petition is not presented, or being presented is withdrawn, the Local Government Board shall confirm the order.§

(5.) The Local Government Board, on confirming an order, may make such modifications therein as they consider necessary for carrying into effect the objects of the order.

(6.) An order under this section, when confirmed by the Local Government Board, shall be forthwith laid upon the table of both Houses of Parliament, if Parliament be then sitting, and, if not, forthwith after the then next meeting of Parliament.||

* But this does not apply to a grouping order under the Local Government Act, 1894, nor to an order establishing or dissolving a parish council or dissolving a group, or other order within section 40 of that Act.

† See section 41 of the Act of 1894.

‡ See subsections (7) and (10) of section 36 of the Local Government Act, 1894, as to parish councils, parish meetings, and guardians petitioning.

§ The validity of an order under this section which has been confirmed by the Department cannot be questioned after six months from the date of confirmation (s. 42 of the Act of 1894).

|| The order does not require the assent or confirmation of Parliament; but an address to the Crown to disallow the order might be moved in either House.

(7.) This section shall be in addition to, and not in derogation of, any power of the Local Government Board in respect of the union or division or alteration of parishes.*

58.—*Additional Power of Local Government Board as to Unions.*—The Local Government Board, where it appears expedient so to do with reference to any poor-law union which is situate in more than one county, instead of dissolving the union, may by order provide that the same shall continue to be one union for the purposes of indoor paupers or any of those purposes, and shall be divided into two or more poor-law unions for the purpose of outdoor relief, and may by the order make such provisions as seem expedient for determining all other matters in relation to which such union is to be one union or two or more unions.†

59.—*Supplemental Provisions as to Alteration of Areas.*—(1.) A [scheme or] order under this Act may make such administrative and judicial arrangements incidental to or consequential on any alteration of boundaries, authorities, or other matters made by the * * * order as may seem expedient.

* * * * * *

(4.) Any * * * order made in pursuance of this Act may, so far as may seem necessary or proper for the purposes of the * * * order, provide for all or any of the following matters, that is to say:—

> (a) may provide for the abolition, restriction, or establishment, or extension of the jurisdiction of any local authority in or over any part of the area affected by the * * * order, and for the adjustment or alteration of the boundaries of such area, and for the constitution

---

* *e.g.*, under the Divided Parishes Act.

† *See* section 36 (6) of the Local Government Act, 1894, as to county councils making orders under this section.

of the local authorities therein, and may deal with the powers and duties of any council, local authorities, quarter sessions, justices of the peace, coroners, sheriff, lieutenant, custos rotulorum, clerk of the peace, and other officer therein, and with the cost of any such authorities, sessions, persons, or officers as aforesaid, and may determine the status of any such area as a component part of any larger area, and provide for the election of representatives in such area, and may extend to any altered area the provisions of any local Act which were previously in force in a portion of the area; and

(b) may make temporary provision for meeting the debts and liabilities of the various authorities affected by the * * * order, for the management of their property, and for regulating the duties, position and remuneration of officers affected by the * * * order, and applying to them the provisions of this Act as to existing officers;* and

(c) may provide for the transfer of any writs, process, records, and documents relating to or to be executed in any part of the area affected by the * * * order, and for determining questions arising from such transfer; and

(d) may provide for all matters which appear necessary or proper for bringing into operation and giving full effect to the * * * order; and

(e) may adjust any property, debts and liabilities affected by the * * * order.

(5.) Where an alteration of boundaries of a county is made by this Act, an order for any of the above

---

* *See* s. 120 of the Act of 1888, *post.*

mentioned matters may, if it appears to the Local Government Board desirable, be made by that Board, but such order, if petitioned against by any council, sessions, or local authority affected thereby, within three months after notice of such order is given in accordance with this Act, shall be provisional only, unless the petition is withdrawn or the order is confirmed by Parliament.

(6.) A [scheme or] order may be made for amending any * * * order previously made in pursuance of this Act, and may be made by the same authority and after the same procedure as the original * * * order. Where a provision of this Act respecting a [scheme or] order requires the * * * order to be laid before Parliament, or to be confirmed by Parliament, either in every case or if it is petitioned against, such * * * order may amend any local and personal Act.

120.—*Compensation to Existing Officers.**—(1.) Every existing officer declared by this Act to be entitled to compensation, and every other existing officer, whether before mentioned in this Act or not, who by virtue of this Act, or anything done in pursuance of or in consequence of this Act, suffers any direct pecuniary loss by abolition of office or by diminution or loss of fees or salary, shall be entitled to have compensation paid to him for such pecuniary loss by the county council, to whom the powers of the authority, whose officer he was, are transferred under this Act, regard being had to the conditions on which his appointment was made, to the nature of his office or employ-

---

* Section 81 of the Local Government Act, 1894, applies this section to the case of existing officers affected by that Act "as if references in [this] section to the county council were references to the parish council, or the district council, or board of guardians, or other authority whose officer the person affected is when the claim for compensation arises, as the case may require."

ment, to the duration of his service, to any additional emoluments which he acquires by virtue of this Act, or of anything done in pursuance of or in consequence of this Act, and to the emoluments which he might have acquired if he had not refused to accept any office offered by any council or other body acting under this Act, and to all the other circumstances of the case, and the compensation shall not exceed the amount which, under the Acts and rules relating to Her Majesty's Civil Service, is paid to a person on abolition of office.

(2.) Every person who is entitled to compensation, as above mentioned, shall deliver to the county council a claim under his hand setting forth the whole amount received and expended by him or his predecessors in office, in every year during the period of five years next before the passing of this Act, on account of the emoluments for which he claims compensation, distinguishing the offices in respect of which the same have been received, and accompanied by a statutory declaration under the Statutory Declaration Act, 1835, that the same is a true statement according to the best of his knowledge, information, and belief.

(3.) Such statement shall be submitted to the county council, who shall forthwith take the same into consideration and assess the just amount of compensation (if any), and shall forthwith inform the claimant of their decision.

(4.) If a claimant is aggrieved by the refusal of the county council to grant any compensation, or by the amount of compensation assessed, or if not less than one-third of the members of such council subscribe a protest against the amount of the compensation as being excessive, the claimant or any subscriber to such protest (as the case may be) may, within three months after the decision of the council, appeal to the Treasury, who shall consider the case and determine whether any compensation, and if so, what amount ought to be granted to the claimant, and such determination shall be final.

(5.) Any claimant under this section, if so required by any member of the county council, shall attend at a meeting of the council and answer upon oath, which any justice present may administer, all questions asked by any member of the council touching the matters set forth in his claim, and shall further produce all books, papers, and documents in his possession or under his control relating to such claim.

(6.) The sum payable as compensation to any person in pursuance of this section shall commence to be payable at the date fixed by the council on granting the compensation, or, in case of appeal, by the Treasury, and shall be a specialty debt due to him from the county council, and may be enforced accordingly in like manner as if the council had entered into a bond to pay the same.

(7.) If a person receiving compensation in pursuance of this section is appointed to any office under the same or any other county council, or by virtue of this Act, or anything done in pursuance of or in consequence of this Act, receives any increase of emoluments of the office held by him, he shall not, while receiving the emoluments of that office, receive any greater amount of his compensation (if any) than, with the emoluments of the said office, is equal to the emoluments for which compensation was granted to him; and if the emoluments of the office he holds are equal to or greater than the emoluments for which compensation was granted, his compensation shall be suspended while he holds such office.

(8.) [All expenses incurred by a district council, in pursuance of this section, shall be paid as general expenses of the council, and any expenses incurred by a board of guardians in pursuance of this section shall be paid out of their common fund, and any expenses incurred by any other authority in pursuance of this section shall be paid out of the fund applicable to payment of the salary of the offices affected.*]

* The words in brackets are from section 81 (7) of the Act of 1894.

INDEX

ACCOUNTS—
    Of charities, 138
    — parish meeting, 195
    — parish council, 195
    — district council, 195
    — county council, 202
    — joint committee, 195
    Inspection of, 197

ACTION—
    Pending, 226

ADJUSTMENT—
    Of property, debts and liabilities, 204

ADOPTIVE ACTS—
    Adoption, 117, 190
    Transfer of powers under, 117, 190, 201
    Expenses, 118, 133
    Borrowing under, 135

ALDERSHOT, 198

ALLOTMENTS—
    Transfer of powers to parish council, 115, 116, 136
    Meetings as to, 110
    Purchase and hiring of land, 122, 128
    Letting, 130

APPOINTED DAY, 221

ARBITRATION—
    On acquisition of land for allotments, 125, 128
    — adjustment of property and liabilities, 205

AREAS—
    Adjustment and alteration, 165, 191, 206, 221

ASSISTANT OVERSEERS—
    Appointment, &c., 112, 145
    — by guardians abolished, 219
    To be officer of parish council, 141, 219

AUDIT—
    Of accounts, 195, 224

AUDITORS—
    District, audit by, 196
    (London), qualification and election, 161, 182
    — existing, continuance in office of, 216

BATHS AND WASHHOUSES ACTS, 117

BOROUGH—
    Council of, a district council, 150
    Appointment of overseers and assistant overseers, 163
    Transfer of powers to council or other representative body, 163, 164
    (New), creation of, effect on parish, 191

BORROWING POWERS—
    Of parish council, 132, 133
    — county council, 135, 202
    For purposes of adjustment, 206

BOUNDARIES—
  Adjustment and alteration, 165, 191, 206, 221
BURIAL ACTS, 117, 201
BYE-LAWS—
  As to recreation grounds, &c., 119
  Existing, continued, 226
CANDIDATES—
  Nomination and election, 182
  Meetings, use of school and other rooms, 111
  For parish council, heckling, 230
  — — —, disqualification of, may be removed, 180
CASUAL VACANCY—
  Filling of, 182, 185, 231
CHAIRMAN—
  Of parish meeting, 107, 144, 178
  — parish council, 109, 181
  — guardians, 149, 197
  — district council, 150, 152, 197
  — metropolitan vestry or district board, 161, 162
CHARITIES, 113, 136, 144, 163, 211
  Questions, settlement of, 207
CHURCH—
  Property, and affairs of, 113, 114
CHURCHWARDENS—
  Cease to be overseers, 113
  Transfer of powers to parish council, 114
CHURCHYARD, 114
CLERK—
  Of parish council, 141, 219
  — district council, 141
COLLECTOR OF POOR RATES, 144

COMMITTEE—
  Meetings, use of schools, &c., 111
  Of parish meeting, 144
  — parish or district council, 193
  — county council, 111, 121
  Joint, 195
COMMON, 121, 157
COMMON PASTURE, 127
COMPOUNDING—
  Of owners for rates, 164
CONSTRUCTION OF ENACTMENTS—
  As to vestry, overseers, &c., 189
CONTRACTS—
  For sewerage and water supply, 140
  Pending, 226
COUNTY BOROUGHS—
  Application of Act to, 161
COUNTY COUNCIL—
  Powers of, in default of district council, 139, 146, 158, 201
  — —, as to areas and boundaries, 165
  Duty of, to bring Act into operation, 221
  Lending by, 135
  May act through district council, 203
  Orders of, to be sent to Government departments, 203
COUNTY RATE—
  Appeals, 114
COUNTY RATE BASIS—
  Appeals, 115
COURT—
  Settlement by, of questions, 207

INDEX.

CURRENT RATES—
  Saving for, 204
DEBTS AND LIABILITIES—
  Transfer of, 204
  Adjustment of, 204
  Existing, saving for, 205
DEFINITIONS, 210
DEMAND NOTES, 133
DIFFICULTIES—
  Power of county council to remove, 185, 217
DISTRICT AUDITOR—
  Audit by, 196
DISTRICT BOARDS—
  (London), 161
DISTRICT COUNCILS—
  Defined, 149
  Powers and duties of, 123, 154
  — — — delegation, 139
  Employment of, by county council, 203
  Failure to perform duty, 127, 139, 144, 158, 201
  Expenses, 159
  See also "Rural District Council," "Urban District Council."
DISTRICT COUNCILLORS—
  See "Rural District Councillors," "Urban District Councillors."
DOCUMENTS—
  Of parish, custody of, 141, 167
ELECTION—
  Of parish councillors, 108, 182
  — guardians, 147, 182
  — district councillors, 151, 152, 182
  — vestrymen and auditors (metropolis), 161, 182
  Expenses, 184
  First, provisions as to, 214

EMIGRANT RUNNERS, 158
EXHAUSTED PARISH LANDS, 180
EXISTING OFFICERS, 218
EXTENT OF ACT, 213
FAIRS, 158
FIRE-ENGINE, 115
FOOTPATHS, 135 (see also "Right of Way")
GAME-DEALERS, 158
GANG-MASTERS, 158
GROUPING OF PARISHES, 103, 170
GUARDIANS—
  Number, 198
  Qualification, 147
  Disqualification, 178
  Election, 147, 182, 200, 217
  Co-optation, 149
  Term of office, resignation and retirement, 148, 185, 199, 214
  Transfer of powers to parish council, 115
  Chairman, 149, 197
  Meetings and proceedings, 197
  Existing, continuance in office, 215
  Where local Act in force, 200
HARBOUR—
  Saving for powers of improvement commission, 203
HIGH COURT—
  Settlement by, of questions, 207
HIGHWAY AUTHORITIES—
  Transfer of powers to district council, 154
HIGHWAY BOARDS—
  abolished, 154
  Existing members of, continuance in office, 215

HIGHWAYS—
    Control of, in rural district, 154
    Stopping diversion, etc., 135, 145
    Expenses, 160, 220
HOUSING OF THE WORKING CLASSES, 116
IMPROVEMENT COMMISSION—
    Harbour powers, 203
INFANT LIFE PROTECTION, 158
INN—
    Use of, for meetings, 200
INQUIRIES, 110, 208
JOINT COMMITTEE, 195
JUSTICES—
    Chairman of councils, &c., are, 150, 162
    Transfer of powers of, 158, 162
KNACKERS' YARDS, 158
LAND—
    Acquisition of, 119, 122, 124
LEGAL PROCEEDINGS—
    Pending, 224, 226
LIGHTING AND WATCHING ACT, 117
LISTS OF VOTERS—
    Preparation of, 175, 222
LITERARY AND SCIENTIFIC INSTITUTIONS ACT, 188
LOCAL GOVERNMENT BOARD—
    Inquiries, &c., by, 110, 208
    Powers of, as to alterations of areas and boundaries, 167
    — —, as to adjustment of property, debts and liabilities, 205
    — —, as to compulsory acquisition of land, 123, 124
    Rules of, for elections, 109, 148, 151, 152, 161, 182

LONDON—
    Provisions as to, 161, 162
MARRIED WOMAN—
    Qualification of, for election, 108, 147, 151, 152, 161
    — —, as voter, 174
NAME—
    of parish or group of parishes or district, 109, 154, 170, 193
NOMINATION—
    of councillors, &c., 182
NOTICES—
    of parish councils and parish meetings, 187, 229
NUISANCES, 120
OFFICERS—
    Existing, 218
    of parish council, 140
OPEN SPACES, 119
OVERSEERS—
    Appointment, 112, 144, 163, 187
    Transfer of powers of, 114, 163
    and chairman of parish meeting incorporated, 145
OWNERS—
    Rating of, 164
OXFORD, 200
PARISH—
    Name of, 109, 193
    Alteration, division, &c., of, 165
    Rural, defined, 106
    — (small), parish meetings in, 144
    books and documents, 115, 141
    chest, 115
    office, 115

INDEX. 249

PARISH—
  property, 113, 115, 145, 170, 194
  wards, 143, 199
PARISH COUNCIL—
  Establishment, 105, 171, 172
  Election, constitution and incorporation of, 108, 182
  Chairman, 109, 141
  Officers, 140
  Meetings and proceedings, 109, 110, 200, 231
  Powers, 112
  Acts of, how signified: consent of parish meeting to, 110, 170, 171
  Expenses, 132
  Failure to elect, 182
  Casual vacancy, 182, 231
  Dissolution, 172
PARISH COUNCILLORS—
  Number, 108
  Qualification, 108
  Disqualification, 178
  Election, 103, 143, 182
  Term of office, resignation, and retirement, 109, 181, 214
PARISH MEETINGS—
  Establishment and constitution, 105, 107
  Chairman, 108, 178
  Time and place of meeting, 107, 110, 177
  Who may convene, 178
  Voting at, 107
  Powers, 117, 132, 136, 188
  Expenses of, and of polls, 108 111, 133, 146
  In large parishes, 143
  — small parishes, 144
  — parts of parishes, 118, 170, 186
  First, provisions as to, 213
PAROCHIAL COMMITTEE, 139

PAROCHIAL ELECTORS—
  defined, 107, 210
  Register of, 174
  Right of, to inspect accounts and documents, 197
  — —, to use school and other rooms, 110
PASSAGE BROKERS, 158
PAWNBROKERS, 158
PETROLEUM ACT—
  Execution of, 158
POLLS—
  consequent on parish meetings, conduct of, 108, 186
  — expenses, 108, 133
POOR RATE—
  Appeals, 114
PROPERTY—
  Transfer and adjustment of, 204
PUBLIC IMPROVE TS ACT, 1860, 117
PUBLIC LIBRARIES ACT, 117
PUBLIC OFFICES, 119
PUBLIC PROPERTY AND CHARITIES, 136
PUBLIC WALKS, 119
QUESTIONS—
  Settlement of, unde Act, 207
RECREATION GROUND, 119, 136, 194
REGISTRATION OF VOTERS, 174
REPEAL OF ACTS, 226
RETURNING OFFICERS, 183, 216
RIGHT OF WAY—
  Acquisition, 120
  Stopping or diversion, 135, 145, 157

INDEX.

ROADSIDE WASTES, 156

RULES—
    as to parish meetings, 229, 233
    — —, parish councils, 231, 233
    — —, committees, 233
    — —, elections, 100, 148, 151, 152, 161, 182

RURAL DISTRICT—
    Alteration, division, &c., and change of name, 165, 193

RURAL DISTRICT COUNCIL—
    Named, change of name, 150, 193
    Constitution and election, 152, 182
    Meetings and proceedings, 197, 200
    Powers of, 139, 154
    Expenses, 159
    Failure to elect, 198
    — to perform duty, 139, 157

RURAL DISTRICT COUNCILLORS—
    Number and qualification, 152
    Disqualification, 178
    Election, 152, 182
    Nomination, 153
    Term of office, resignation and retirement, 152, 185, 199, 214

RURAL PARISH—
    What is a, 106

RURAL SANITARY AUTHORITY—
    Existing members of, continuance in office, 215

SCHOOL—
    Use of, for meetings, 110
    Saving for, 203

SCHOOL BOARD—
    Formation and dissolution, 188

SCHOOL SITES ACT, 188

SCILLY ISLANDS, 210

SECURITIES—
    Existing, 225

SEWERAGE, 139

SHORT TITLE OF ACT, 213

TREASURER—
    of parish council, 141

TRUSTEES—
    of charities 136

URBAN DISTRICT—
    Creation or extension of, effect on parish, 191
    Change of name, 193
    Appointment of overseers and assistant overseers, 163
    Transfer of powers to district council or other body, 163, 164

URBAN DISTRICT COUNCIL—
    Named, change of name, 150, 193
    Constitution and election, 150, 182
    Meetings and proceedings, 197, 200
    Powers of, 154
    Expenses, 159
    Failure to elect, 198
    — — perform duty, 158, 201
    Transfer to, of powers under Adoptive Acts, 201

URBAN DISTRICT COUNCILLORS—
    Qualification, 151
    Disqualification, 178
    Election, 151, 182
    Term of office, resignation and retirement, 151, 182, 214

URBAN SANITARY AUTHORITY—
   Existing members of, continuance in office, 216

VALUATION LIST, 114, 225

VESTRY—
   Transfer of powers to parish meeting, 144
   — — parish council, 113
   (London), appointment of overseers and assistant overseers, &c., transfer of powers, 163, 164

VESTRY CLERK, 141, 218

VESTRYMEN—
   (London) qualification and election, 161, 182
   — existing, continuance of, in office, 216

VESTRY ROOM, 115

VICE-CHAIRMAN—
   of guardians, 149, 197
   of district council, 197

VILLAGE GREENS, 115, 119

VOTING—
   at parish meetings, 107
   at elections under Act, 107, 148, 151, 152, 161

WATER SUPPLY, 120, 139

WOMEN—
   Married, *see* "Married Women"

WOOLWICH, 161, 184, 216

Woodfall & Kinder, Printers, 70 to 76, Long Acre, W.C.

LAW AND POLITICS.

The undermentioned Books are by W. A. HOLDSWORTH, Esq.

- **1/-** Practical Family Lawyer. 2nd Edition, embodying all the Changes in the Law. 640 pages.
- **2/6** County Court Guide: A Handbook of Practice and Procedure, with Useful Forms and Table of Fees and Costs. 1881.
- **2/6** Handy Book of Parish Law. 10th Edition, 1886, comprising all New Legislation up to date.
- **2/6** Bankruptcy Act of 1883, and Bankruptcy Rules; in One Volume.
- **1/-** Law of Landlord and Tenant, with a Collection of Useful Forms. 35th Edition, 1886, including all recent Statutes.
- **1/-** The Agricultural Holdings (England) Act 1883, and the Ground Game Act 1880. New Edition. With an Appendix of Forms, etc., and an Index. 1888.
- **1/-** The Allotments Acts, 1887, with the Cottage Gardens Compensation Act, 1887, and the Allotments Act of 1882.
- **1/-** Bankruptcy Act of 1883. Seventh Edition, with new matter. Viz.
    The Debtors' Act, 1869.
    Bankruptcy Appeals (County Courts) Act, 1884.
    Bankruptcy (Agricultural Labourers' Wages) Act, 1886.
    The Rules as to Administration Orders.
- **1/-** Bankruptcy Rules, 1883, and the General Rules as to Administration Orders, Forms, Scale of Costs, Fees, etc.
- **1/-** Corrupt and Illegal Practices Prevention Act, 1883, and the unrepealed Provisions of the Acts 1854, 1875.
- **1/-** Weights and Measures' Acts.
- **1/-** Ballot Act, 1872, for Parliamentary and Municipal Elections.
- **1/-** Law of Wills, Executors, etc.
- **1/-** Married Women's Property Act.

Law and Politics—*continued.*

1/- Voter's Guide and Canvasser's Manual, a Popular Explanation of the Law relating to Elections, 1885.   J. TREVOR DAVIES.

1/- Handbook of Parliamentary Procedure, for the Use of Local Parliaments and Debating Societies.   H. W. LUCY.

1/6 History of Reform of the Representation of the People in Parliament, including Details of the Franchise, Seats, and Registration Acts. 5th Edition, Enlarged.   ALEX. PAUL.

3/6 An Inquiry into the Nature and Causes of the Wealth of Nations. Unabridged. 780 pages.   ADAM SMITH.

1/6 Ireland's Disease: Letters written to "Le Temps." Translated by the Author.   PHILIPPE DARYL.

Volumes on Politics in MORLEY'S UNIVERSAL LIBRARY.

1/-, cloth, cut edges; 1/-, cloth, uncut edges; 1/6, parchment back.

Two Speeches on Conciliation with America and Two Letters on Irish Questions.   EDMUND BURKE.

Leviathan; or, The Matter, Form, and Power of a Commonwealth, Ecclesiastical and Civil.   THOMAS HOBBES.

Two Treatises on Civil Government.   LOCKE.

{ Patriarcha; or, The Power of Kings.   Sir ROBERT FILMER.
{ The Prince; The Life of Castracani, etc.   MACHIAVELLI.

Ideal Commonwealths, More's Utopia, Bacon's New Atlantis, &c.

Commonwealth of Oceana.   HARRINGTON.

On Government.   ARISTOTLE.

POLITICAL SPEECHES.

6/-, paper covers; 1/6, in cloth; 3/6, with Portrait.

The Right Hon. W. E. Gladstone's Speeches.

The Right Hon. Joseph Chamberlain's Speeches.

The Marquis of Salisbury's Speeches.

Lord Randolph Churchill's Speeches.

AGRICULTURE AND FARMING.

12/6   The Horse in the Stable and in the Field: Varieties, Management in Health and Disease, Anatomy, Physiology, etc. 160 Illustrations.   (STONEHENGE.)   J. H. WALSH.

1/-   The Horse. Varieties, Management, &c. Illus. by WELLS. CECIL.

2/6   The Stud Farm. On Breeding for the Turf, the Chase, and the Road. Cloth.   CECIL.

2/-   ——————— Boards.   Ditto.

5/-   How to Farm Profitably. (1st Series.) The Speeches and Writings of Mr. MECHI.

3/6   The Farmer's Harvest Companion and Country Gentleman's Assistant.   T. JARVIS and W. BURNESS.

2/-   Our Farm of Four Acres.

1/6   Scientific Farming Made Easy.   T. C. FLETCHER.

1/6   Agricultural Chemistry.   A. SIBSON.

1/-   Food, Feeding, and Manure.   Ditto.

1/-   Hints and Facts for Farmers.   R. SCOTT BURN.

1/-   Cattle: Their Breeds, Management, etc.; The Dairy.   W. C. L. MARTIN.

1/-   Bees: Their Habits, Management, etc.   Rev. J. G. WOOD.

2/-   British Timber Trees.   JOHN BLENKARN.

1/6   Mushroom Culture. 38 Illustrations.   W. ROBINSON.

1/-   London Market Gardens: How to Grow Flowers, Fruits, and Vegetables for Profit.   W. SHAW.

1/-   The Apple in Orchard and Garden: An Account of its Improved Culture. With a Chapter on Apple Cookery.   J. GROOM.

1/-   Asparagus Culture: the Best Methods employed in England and France. Particulars of the Seven Years' Competition.   J. BARNES and W. ROBINSON.

1/-   The Potato in Farm and Garden: Every phase of its Cultivation, with Chapters on the Disease of the Potato.   R. FREMLIN.

1/-   Fruit Culture for Profit: The Profitable Cultivation of Sixteen Kinds of Fruit.   E. HOBDAY.

1/-   Flax and Hemp. Culture and Manipulation.   E. S. DELAMER

1/-   Agriculture: Its History, Importance, and Prospects.   JUDGE HASTINGS INGHAM.

FLOWERS AND PLANTS.

5/-	Garden Botany. 20 pages of Coloured Illusts.	AGNES CATLOW.
5/-	Greenhouse Botany. 20 pages of Coloured Illusts.	Ditto.
3/6	Gardening at a Glance. Many Illustrations.	GEORGE GLENNY.
2/-	——————————— Cheaper Edition.	Ditto.
2/-	Hardy Shrubs. Woodcuts and Coloured Plates.	W. D. PRIOR.
1/-	Town Gardening: A Handbook of Trees, Shrubs, and Plants, suitable for Town Cultivation in the Out-door Garden, Window Garden, and Greenhouse.	R. C. RAVENSCROFT.
1/-	The Kitchen Garden. Roots, Vegetables, Herbs, and Fruits.	E. S. DELAMER.
1/-	The Flower Garden. Bulbous, Tuberous, Fibrous, Rooted, and Shrubby Flowers.	E. S. DELAMER.
3/6	The Kitchen Garden and The Flower Garden in one volume, gilt edges.	E. S. DELAMER.
1/-	The Cottage Garden. How to Lay it out, and Cultivate it to Advantage.	ANDREW MEIKLE.
3/6	Roses, and How to Grow Them. Coloured Plates.	W. D. PRIOR.
1/6	——————————— Cheaper Edition.	Ditto.
3/6	Wild Flowers: Where to Find, and How to Know Them, with 12 Coloured Plates by NOEL HUMPHREYS, and many Woodcuts.	Dr. S. THOMSON.
2/-	———— Plain Plates.	Ditto.
3/6	Haunts of the Wild Flowers. Coloured Plates and many Woodcuts	ANNE PRATT.
3/6	Woodlands, Heaths, and Hedges. Many Coloured Plates.	W. S. COLEMAN.
1/-	——————————— Plain Plates.	Ditto.
5/-	History of British Ferns. 22 pages of Coloured Illusts.	T. MOORE.
3/6	British Ferns and their Allies—the Club-Mosses, Pepperworts, and Horsetails. Coloured Plates by COLEMAN.	T. MOORE.
1/-	——— ———— Cheaper Edition. Coloured Plates.	Ditto.
5/-	Profitable Plants: used for Food, Clothing, Medicine, etc. 20 pages of Coloured Illustrations.	T. C. ARCHER.
5/-	Palms and their Allies. 20 pages of Coloured Illustrations.	Dr. B. SEEMANN.
5/-	British Mosses. 20 pages of Coloured Illustrations.	R. STARK.
3/6	The Family Doctor. 500 Illustrations, comprising all the Medicinal Plants.	

UNIVERSITY OF CALIFORNIA LIBRARY
Los Angeles

This book is DUE on the last date stamped below.

Form L9-25m-9,'47(A5618)444